Away From Home

A Short History of Provision for Separated Children

R. A. Parker

A Barnardo's Practice Paper
1990

ISBN 0 902046 07 1

Published by
Barnardo's, Tanners Lane, Barkingside
Ilford, Essex IG6 1QG

Typeset, printed and bound by Barnardo Print Training Scheme, Hertford, Herts

Barnardo Practice Paper

Barnardo's is a Christian based voluntary child care organization, which seeks to work in partnership with parents, local authorities and central government to provide community-based services for families with preschool children, children who have a mental handicap and young people in trouble or who are unemployed. Also it provides a range of specialised family placement services for 'hard to place' youngsters including delinquent adolescents and children with a handicap. Residential services consist of special boarding schools, community homes with education, units for children who have a severe mental handicap and adolescents unable to live at home. The eight child care divisions are situated in disadvantaged areas in England (5), Scotland, Ireland, and Wales.

As a national voluntary organisation, Barnardo's has the advantage of encompassing a variety of settings and methods in the care of children and families. With this advantage we acknowledge the linked obligation to make known our work and to share our thinking and experience.

Acknowledgements

I am grateful to Barnardo's, and especially to Nora Dixon, for suggesting that I should write this book and for providing the necessary financial assistance. The ideas and interpretations that it contains have been fostered by the work of many people over many years. It is impossible to thank them all by name, but I do thank them collectively most sincerely. However, I must mention the special help and encouragement that I have received from those generous present and former colleagues at the University of Bristol who have shared with me a long-standing interest in child care and especially in its history. I am deeply indebted to all of them. My warmest thanks also go to my colleagues at the Dartington Social Research Unit who have contributed so much to the study of child care, not least by having hosted our regular research seminars for more years than I or they will care to remember. I am also most grateful to Patricia Lees for her assistance and support in the preparation of this material.

Some of the material upon which the book draws (especially in Chapter 4) was assembled in connection with a project on long-term trends in child care that I have been undertaking with my colleague Frank Loughran and which has been supported by the Economic and Social Research Council. My thanks go to him and to the Council.

It goes without saying, however, that none of these colleagues, nor Barnardo's, is responsible for any errors or fanciful interpretations that may be found in what follows: they all belong to me.

Contents

1 Introduction

I Preamble

There is no *single* history of child care, for history is an interpretation of the past that depends first upon the questions that we pose, and, secondly, upon the perspective that we bring to bear upon our explanations. In both senses it is selective – a selectivity that is itself superimposed upon the incomplete nature of the source material that has survived. The most accessible records were generally written by administrators and dealt with broad issues. Furthermore, they were often carefully constructed in order to present a favourable impression of the work of the organisation. Various archives do contain the records of individual children and, to a lesser extent, their families but these were also compiled for organisational purposes. Ordinary people – and the poor and children in particular – have left us few written accounts of their experiences.[1] Fortunately, the development of oral history is beginning to redress the balance, although such personal stories can only cover the period of living memory, and tend to be descriptive rather than analytical.[2]

Popular impressions of child care history have been shaped by compelling images, many of which were contrived to enlist public support for this or that cause. Oliver Twist remains the archetypal 19th century waif subjected to a harsh and insensitive workhouse regime – a character and scene Dickens created, at least in part, to reinforce the campaign for the reform of the Poor Law. The 'orphan' and the orphanage have also been prominent in the folklore of child care, even though genuine orphans never formed more than a small minority of children in care, always being outnumbered by the children of lone mothers.

There are other images that are associated with the great philanthropic societies. There are, for example, the powerful 'before and after' photographs that Barnardo used to illustrate the extent to which filthy, ragged and hungry street children had been transformed by admission to his Homes.[3] Indeed, the photograph of the ill-used and pathetic child remains an effective means by which to arouse public sympathy and generosity.

The imagery of child care is important because most of it was (and is) created for a purpose, albeit for different purposes by different interests. It, too, was inevitably selective, for it was intended to simplify and to draw attention to one issue rather than another. These images have their own history, related to the romanticised and sentimental views of childhood that were to become so common in popular Victorian novels, but they are dangerous starting points for a history of child care. That history is both more complex and more diversified than the images convey. In the chapters that follow I have endeavoured to capture some of that complexity and diversity without overwhelming the reader with too much detail and without losing sight of the need to offer explanations that are sufficiently general to be able to account for broad trends, movements and developments.

What I have not done, for want of time and resources, is to describe the experiences of children who, over the last 100 years or so, were separated from their families and brought up under the Poor Law and its successors or by one of the many voluntary children's societies. Even had I been able to assemble the material from which such a picture could have been composed I suspect that it would have revealed wide variations in those experiences – especially in how they were remembered. It is tempting to believe otherwise, for all children 'in care' must have suffered the same feelings of sadness, loneliness and anger at their fate that still remain such poignant emotions for the separated child. Yet beyond such shared emotions there lay many differences in what happened to these children: whether they met with kindness and individual attention or were exposed to cruelty and indifference; whether or not they were with their brothers and sisters; and whether they were trained in a useful occupation or exploited as cheap labour. None of these children was fortunate[4] but, once in care, fortune favoured some more than others, whilst for an unknown number being in care saved them from gross deprivation and abuse.

In what follows there are, therefore, no case studies illustrating these themes, but there are other themes of a different kind. Each chapter deals with a recognisable strand of child care history, such as boarding-out, but these subjects are discussed in such a way that they reveal their relationship with other aspects of child care history. Beyond that, however, they are explored in the context of the numerous socio-economic forces that have shaped child care policy and practice – the primary purpose of this book. Its approach, therefore, is also selective but, as with the contribution of oral history, it employs a perspective that has been comparatively little used and may, thus, help to redress the interpretive balance. It does not pretend to be comprehensive, but the theme of each chapter provides a window on an assortment of other possible themes.

II Interconnections

Unlike its development in a number of other European countries, provision for separated children in Britain has been organised *outside* the education system. There was a short time in the 1850s during which an embryonic central department of education was responsible for the reformatory and industrial schools and another period between 1930 and 1948 when some local authorities assigned their public assistance responsibilities with respect to the care of children to their departments of education. There were, too, junctures at which strong bids were made for the public sector of child care to become an educational responsibility, as happened, for example, in the 1890s during and after the deliberations of the Mundella Committee on poor law children.[5] However, there were several broad reasons why these failed. One was the fact that, by the time that the education system was established, both the Poor Law and the voluntary children's societies had already made provision for the care of separated children. Had popular education been established earlier, the history of child care might have followed a different course. As it was, basic education was provided internally by both the Poor Law and by the voluntary societies ahead of the availability of universal elementary education because of the belief that only through education and training could the cycles of pauperism, deprivation and evil be broken.

It should be noted, however, that the picture of poor law care for children in Scotland was rather different. Unlike England and Wales, no poor relief was available for the able-bodied. There was, therefore, no need for the creation of a workhouse system to test the eligibility of such applicants. As a result, from the outset many more children were boarded-out. Another reason lay in the earlier development of parish systems of education in Scotland. Even where children were in poor law institutions, therefore, it was more common for them to go out to school than to receive their instruction on the premises.

So, the different stages at which public education and child care were established has an important bearing upon the continuing division of the two systems. So too has the sectarian nature of almost all of the main voluntary children's societies that were founded between the 1860s and the 1880s. The problem of denominational education, but especially the separation of Catholics from Protestants, had been a major and highly controversial issue in the creation of public education. Battles were fought, compromises made and bargains struck. In the light of that experience, successive governments were anxious to avoid the reopening of such issues; and this would undoubtedly have occurred had there been any suggestion later that the regulation or financial support of the voluntary children's societies should be placed in the hands of either local or central education authorities. Furthermore, the sectarian divisions between the main children's societies were deep, often bitter and more complicated than simply a discordance between Catholics and Protestants.

A third reason for the detachment of education and child care was the small size of the 'child care' population. It is difficult to calculate how many children were, at any one time, looked after by the Poor Law and the children's societies combined. There was, as we shall see, a good deal of overlap, and although the voluntary sector is generally thought of in terms of some half-dozen or so large national organisations there were hundreds of other small enterprises up and down the country, many of which, until 1933, remained unregistered and, therefore, unrecorded.[6] Nevertheless, it is doubtful whether the total number of children 'in care' at any one time ever exceeded 125,000 during the last 100 years or so. This represents a rate of less than one child in a 100. Thus, by comparison with the population of children of school age, they were a tiny fraction.

However, this was not the only factor that made them peripheral to the general system of education. A substantial proportion (probably as much as a fifth throughout the second half of the 19th century and the first half of this), were detained in the reformatory and industrial schools that became the approved schools after 1933, and community homes with education more recently. These were children who, for one reason or another, had been classed as troublesome or 'at risk'. Indeed, after the establishment of compulsory elementary education at the end of the 1870s the industrial schools were used as a form of punishment for those children who persisted in not attending school. Even now children are committed to local authority care for persistent truancy. Thus, children who could not be satisfactorily incorporated in the mainstream of education were directed outwards to the care system. It became, therefore, a useful facility for state education precisely because it *was* separate.

Finally, children in care remained politically peripheral to the main education system because, when opportunities arose for the education authorities to take over the care services, they were frequently preoccupied with major educational reforms. This was particularly apparent in the 1940s. The preparation of the Education Act of 1944, but more importantly its subsequent implementation, occurred whilst the future of child care was being fought out between the Home Office and the Ministry of Health. By 1947, when the groundwork for the reform of education had been completed, it was too late for the Ministry of

Education to bid successfully for child care responsibilities – even though, by then, it was anxious to do so.[7]

Administratively, education and child care have thus gone their separate ways. However, as we shall see, the histories of the two systems were interwoven in important respects. The division of administrative responsibility should not obscure the impact that developments in education have had upon the evolution of child care – as a result, for example, of the raising of the school-leaving age or the chequered history of nursery school provision.

Similar conclusions can be drawn about the penal system, and the effect on child care of the changes that occurred in the way in which juvenile offenders were defined (for example, in terms of the age of criminal responsibility) and dealt with. It was, for instance, the quest to keep children away from the contaminating influences of prison which provided much of the impetus for the foundation of reformatory and industrial schools. It was the introduction of probation, in 1907, that enabled magistrates to avoid sending certain youngsters to prison. Furthermore, in the following year, the establishment of separate juvenile courts gradually created a magistracy that was more experienced in dealing with children and more sympathetic towards them.

Other examples could be used to illustrate the theme of interconnections: such as the connection between child care and the juvenile labour market, and that between child care and the health services. For instance, the rapid growth of residential nurseries during the Second World War was under the general direction of the Ministry of Health, even though it used a variety of voluntary organisations, including the established children's societies, as its agents. By the beginning of 1946 there was a peak of some 12,000 children in these nurseries, but by the end of that year fewer than 2,000.[8] Clearly, both the rise and fall of this form of full-time residential care for young children left its mark upon the fortunes of the voluntary sector as children (and the money to pay for their care) first flowed in and then rapidly ebbed away. Beyond that however, the fact that nursery care was seen as an extension of medical care left its mark upon the assumptions that were made about how babies and toddlers should be looked after.

Yet it would be misleading simply to draw attention to interconnections such as these between different services, important though they are. What is more enlightening is to see how policies and practices in child care (of which these services were the manifestation) were shaped by larger socio-economic factors and forces.

III Shaping forces

There were many wider forces that influenced the evolution of child care during the last century or so, but a number will make their appearance several times in the chapters that follow. Here, by way of introduction, we touch briefly upon some of the more significant of them.

Industrialisation

The industrialisation of Britain in the 19th century was of profound importance. Not only did it transform methods of production but it brought with it other far-reaching economic and social changes. Wage labour became virtually universal, creating a working-class that was deeply vulnerable to the periodic recessions in trade that characterised the emergent capitalist economy. Domestic forms of production were replaced by factory employment in which cheap child labour was at first actively sought and later, with the advent of more sophisticated technology, largely discarded (even though it survived longer in some industries, like textiles, than in others). Industrialisation also created wealth that was not based upon land ownership. A new and larger middle class emerged which, amongst other things, clamoured for domestic servants – a demand which, when the time came for girls to leave care, absorbed almost all of them. The new wealth also facilitated the surge of charitable giving which was associated with the religious revivalism that provided so much of the energy that lay behind the formation of voluntary children's organisations of all kinds.

Supporting the British Empire

Britain's economic growth in the 19th century depended heavily upon its extensive empire which provided cheap raw materials and a protected market for exported manufactured goods. A large standing Army and Navy were crucial to the protection of overseas possessions and to ensure that the sea routes were kept open for British trade. Many boys who had been brought up under the Poor Law or by the children's societies found employment in the armed forces or in the merchant navy. Indeed, the 'ship schools' became a notable feature of the provision for separated boys. The sparsely populated countries of the British Empire also needed to be settled in order to be developed, not least as markets for home production. Canada and Australia in particular received many thousands of separated British children who were emigrated by the voluntary societies, a process facilitated by the development of steamships and subsidies of various kinds.

Urbanisation

Another consequence of industrialisation was urbanisation. Thousands flooded into the cities from the countryside, partly pulled and partly pushed by the changing balance between manufacture and agriculture. Towns grew rapidly, accompanied by overcrowding, homelessness and the disruption of families and communities. The population of Greater London, for example, increased from one million at the start of the 19th century to six and a half million at the end. In the last 50 years of that century the population of Liverpool multiplied nearly tenfold.[9] Poor quality housing was built down to the rent that wage labourers could pay; the slums proliferated. With such rapid urbanisation and low wages went a concentration of population that increased the visibility of poverty and deprivation, arousing the spectre of social disorder – if not, indeed, of revolution.

Disease and disability

Disease followed in the wake of urban congestion. Epidemics, such as the cholera outbreak that swept through East London in the late 1860s, left children without one parent or both. Tuberculosis too spread swiftly, especially amongst children. Indeed, throughout the 19th century and into the first decades of the 20th century, it was commonplace for children to die. Diseases such as diphtheria exacted a fearful toll and vaccination and immunisation did not become widespread until the 1930s. Rates of infant mortality remained high until the second decade of this century. For example, the rate of deaths of infants under 1 year per 1,000 live births in England and Wales was 162 in 1850, 158 in 1875 and 154 in 1900. A marked drop did not begin until 1919 and it was not until 1925 that the 1850 rate was halved.[10] Even then (as now), it continued to be disproportionately high in impoverished areas. It is easy to appreciate the desire of many social reformers to rescue children from the squalor and danger of densely populated, poverty-stricken and unhealthy environments, just as much as from the danger of the factory or the prison.[11] Indeed, the treatment of diseases such as tuberculosis and the prevention of their spread were considered to require the segregation of the sufferers in, for example, fresh-air hospitals.

Familiarity with child mortality is one of the important backgrounds against which attitudes towards children and their treatment have to be understood. When infant and child deaths were so common, it was often difficult to differentiate between those that were attributable to deliberate ill-treatment and those which were not. Likewise, when many poor children were malnourished, and suffered from such associated diseases

as rickets, neglect was a more elusive concept than it is today. Furthermore, the accident rate amongst children was also much higher. Children
and youngsters who worked long hours with dangerous machinery were
frequently maimed, whilst home accidents – from suffocation through
being overlain in their parents' bed to burns from open fires – were
common enough tragedies to be regarded as unexceptional. Other children
were born with deformities or handicaps, some of which were congenital
but many more attributable to the poor standard of their mother's health
and nutrition during pregnancy. It comes as something of a surprise today
to realise how many special Homes there were in the past for crippled
children, delicate children, for children with TB, or for children who were
deaf, dumb or blind.

Population fluctuations

Other demographic statistics as well as those concerned with infant
mortality and morbidity have had a bearing on the history of child care.
There are, of course, the changes in the birth rate and the associated
changes in the size and age structure of the child population. For example,
as the adolescent population becomes larger or smaller the number of
juvenile delinquents has usually varied accordingly. The number of
illegitimate births (and subsequent abandonment) has also influenced the
demand for child care, not least because for most of the last 100 years
the severe economic problems faced by single mothers have been
compounded by social stigma and unsympathetic treatment by those
organisations to which they were obliged to turn for help.[12]

The enormous number of male deaths in the 1914–18 war represents
another kind of demographic change which also made its mark on child
care. Many women were left without the prospect of a partner and,
therefore, with the problem of making a life in a male-dominated society.
The position of single women in the housing market was extremely weak
and that of women generally in the labour market was economically
depressed. As a result, the large cohort of single women produced by
the ever-growing casualty lists provided an important source of live-in
staff for residential homes for nearly 40 years. Such work (and residential
domestic service) provided the board, lodging and income that was so
difficult for them to obtain in other ways. This example makes plain not
only the importance of demographic factors to child care history but also
that of the state and nature of labour markets.

Some effects of variations in labour markets

Two examples will illustrate the importance of these points. We have
already drawn attention to certain differences between the English and

Scottish Poor Laws that made the development of workhouses less necessary in Scotland. There was, therefore, little institutional accommodation available for the children who needed to be looked after by the Poor Law. Instead, throughout the 19th century, large numbers were boarded-out. For example, in 1890 when detailed returns first became available they showed that 86 per cent of the children in the care of the Scottish boards of guardians were boarded-out.[13] That was made possible partly by boarding them out with relatives (about 40 per cent) but also because of the existence of crofting economies in the Highlands and Islands where another pair of hands could always be used and produce was consumed rather than marketed. Sufficiency crofting made it inexpensive to feed extra mouths, albeit at a frugal level. Furthermore, little money circulated in these economies, so that boarding-out allowances, received regularly in cash, were especially welcome – not least in order to pay rents. In short, there was a buoyant demand for poor law children.

Elsewhere in Britain such economies had virtually disappeared by the 19th century except in parts of Wales, the south west and the English border counties. However, in Canada small family farms predominated (the land grant system usually allocated lots of 160 acres) until the opening up of the prairies. Even then, farmers in the settled areas were still anxious to recruit child labour, for there was often neither the means to pay for regular hired hands nor to invest in the new agricultural machinery. Family labour was crucial and children made an important contribution from an early age. This was the economic opportunity to which the child emigrationists in Britain responded, encouraged by subsidies from the Canadian government. In the 50 years before the First World War, some 80,000 separated children left Britain – mainly for placement on such farms. What was described on this side of the Atlantic as child-saving was seen in Canada as welcome farm labour.[14]

Economic constraints affecting the historical development of child care

There are, of course, many other important economic aspects to child care history. At a more specific level, the manner in which the services for children were financed exercised a powerful influence on what was done or not done. The most obvious example was the preoccupation of the Poor Law with the limitation of expenditure. However, it was not solely a concern about expenditure on children, even though children comprised about a third of all those receiving indoor relief throughout most of the last 100 years of poor law history. What dominated the politics of destitution was the fear that large numbers of the able-bodied, with their dependants in tow, would seek poor relief if given the slightest encouragement to do so. That was the principal anxiety that led to the legislative changes of 1834 which conceived the workhouse and the workhouse test as the major means of combating a rising tide of costly able-bodied destitution. What happened to children, to the sick and to the old who were *not* 'able-bodied' was for long dominated by policies and practices that were directed to the control of those who *were*. The deliberately harsh regimes of the general mixed workhouses were mainly aimed at deterring the able-bodied but, inevitably, affected the lives of all other inmates.

Thus, the gradual separation of children within the poor law system that began to gain momentum in the 1850s was of great importance to the quality of care that they received. Poor law schools, special Homes and scattered cottages all emerged in the process of differentiation, although even in 1946 the Curtis Committee could still report that there was a disturbingly large number of children who were accommodated in public assistance institutions that were intended for adults.[15] Furthermore, despite the provision of separate accommodation and special staff for looking after children, there were many examples of the continued application of the 1834 principles of less eligibility. For instance, boards of guardians were reluctant to spend more on the children in their schools and Homes than might be spent on their children by working parents. If the conditions of children in care were to be seen as better than those of children who were not, it was feared that the floodgates of expenditure would be thrown open – as parents sought to abdicate their responsibilities.

However, it was not only in the sphere of indoor relief that the control and regulation of expenditure through deterrence operated. Both the central authorities[16] and many local boards of guardians were anxious to limit the payment of relief to people in their own homes. One way of doing that was by the close – and often humiliating – scrutiny of the circumstances of each applicant, reinforced by the 'offer of the house'. Many must have been deterred from seeking relief for fear that they would end up in the workhouse or be sent back to their area of settlement, as financial responsibilities were passed between boards of guardians. The position of the many able-bodied but lone mothers presented a particularly worrying problem for the poor law authorities. It seemed clear that such women would not need to be paid outdoor relief if, freed from the care of their children, they could obtain work. Ironically, therefore, in some areas children were admitted to care as an *economising* measure, to enable their mothers to take paid employment.

Against this kind of background it becomes clear why the separation of public child care from the administration of poor relief had such far-reaching consequences. The process began in 1934[17] and was completed by the 1948 Children Act. After that the departments responsible for child care were no longer involved in the assessment and payment of public assistance. Child care policy could be developed independently and free from the long-standing shadow of a poor law system preoccupied with what it saw as the ever-present willingness of people to abuse, or rely unduly upon, relief payments.

The poor rates were not, however, the only source from which child care services had been financed. From the 1850s until just after the First World War the reformatory and industrial schools, run largely by voluntary bodies, were partly financed by the Treasury via the Home Office. The subsidy took the form of a *per capita* grant, which had the effect of encouraging both expansion *and* the retention of children for as long as possible in order to maximise income. A different system of financial support that removed these particular incentives was employed later and served to enhance the power of the Home Office to regulate what the schools did and how they were managed.

The financial influences exerted upon the voluntary children's societies

Few of the voluntary children's societies have depended upon major benefactors. Much of their money has been collected by subscription and from numerous small donations, legacies and endowments. As a result, there was rarely an outside body or individual able to exercise a controlling influence because of the size of their financial contribution. While that allowed the societies a good deal of independence, it gave them little financial security. Their much vaunted autonomy has had less to do with their voluntary status than with the fragmented nature of their income.

Even when, as time passed, they obtained a larger proportion of this income from public bodies, they too were often numerous and unable to exert any co-ordinated influence. This was particularly true of the assortment of boards of guardians (and later, but to a lesser extent, the local authorities) whose children the societies received on a fee-paying basis. Only a central department would have been in a position to make its financial support dependent upon the acceptance of various forms of regulative control and, with the exception of the reformatory and industrial schools, central government did not make those kinds of payments to the voluntary sector.

Financial considerations, and especially the *forms* of income, have influenced the development of child care policies and practices in many ways. They are hard, concrete matters that can usually be verified from the records, since financial transactions are one of the items of information that are systematically noted and filed (at least where they are required to be audited). They may appear dull and complicated but their details cannot be ignored by anyone who is anxious to obtain a grasp of child care history. In contrast, the ideologies that have influenced child care are much less tangible, although in many ways they have been the most powerful of the factors which have determined the way in which child care has developed.

Some ideological influences upon the development of child care

Religious beliefs, particularly those associated with evangelism, provided strong motive forces for many of the initiatives in child care. The cause of child-saving in the 19th century was often indistinguishable from the cause of child salvation. Religious convictions placed a premium upon the moral reclamation of children and gave those who became involved a missionary confidence in what they did that left little room for doubt – and which often manifested itself in a heady mixture of compassion and self-righteousness. At the same time it produced a remarkable level and pool of energy and commitment. The religious revival of the 19th century was a popular movement which attracted people from all walks of life. The voluntary children's societies were thus able to appeal to a broad base of support. Nevertheless, it would be wrong to assume that it was only in the voluntary sector that the religious revival exerted its influence for, particularly at the local level, its impact can be detected in the deliberations of boards of guardians as well as in the attitudes of many of the staff who worked in their institutions. Just as in the voluntary Homes, it was often religious convictions that drew people to such work.

The impact of religious beliefs upon Victorian child care can hardly be overestimated. However, as we shall see, the sectarianism that pervaded this era (and especially the anti-catholicism) led to a variety of interpretations, both personal and denominational, that ranged from a stern and unyielding fundamentalism to a gentle and sensitive compassion. Children who encountered one variety were likely to be looked after quite differently from those who encountered another.

Various quite specific ideas, sometimes associated with these religious interpretations, have exercised strong influences over child care policies and practices. For instance, there was a long period during which children were regarded as essentially malleable, at least as long as they could be removed from detrimental surroundings and pernicious influences. They were thought capable of forgetting the past and making a new start, but that such 'renewal' required conducive environments in which retraining could be accomplished through careful instruction and good example. Given these conditions – best created, it was believed, in residential settings – the course of children's lives could be changed for the better. Today, much of that simple optimism has disappeared, partly because the power of education and treatment is assumed to be more limited, but also because the separation of children from their families and communities is regarded more as a problem than a solution. The ends, even if achievable, are no longer considered to justify the means. For the 19th century child-savers, however, the ends were seen as both achievable and all-important.

Ideological shifts in emphasis
Exactly when and how the belief in the pliability of children came to lose its hold on the ideology of child care is far from clear. Perhaps the turning point came from a combination of the disillusionment with the idea of progress that followed the 1914-18 War and the waning of religious conviction that dated from much the same time. Possibly it occurred later, as a result of the sobering experience of mass evacuation during the Second World War, or from the criticism of institutional forms of care that, although ever-present, intensified during the 1940s. Whatever the reasons, the principle of malleability had lost its dominance in child care by the time of the inauguration of the new children's service in 1948.

Nonetheless, the questions of how it was thought that children's pliability could be exploited, and to what ends, remain of considerable interest, for they help us to understand the nature of the care regimes. For example, it is clear that work was highly valued both as a reforming influence and as a good in itself. Once the habits of regular work had been instilled, the child was believed to wear, as it were, a suit of protective clothing that safeguarded him thereafter. Indeed, it was natural that such ideas should be found in child care for they were also deeply embedded in society at large. Uprightness, moral rectitude and good citizenship were commonly related to the virtue of hard work. Idleness led in the opposite direction. Even for quite young children then, work was an important part of being in care, and regimes were organised accordingly. As well as being viewed as an end in itself, work could also be justified as a useful means of imposing discipline and as training that prepared the child for employment.

Although malleable, children were also considered wayward and prone to misdemeanor. Punishment, and particularly physical punishment, was widely regarded as an appropriate corrective both in society generally and in child care – a fact to which many reports of inquiries into its excessive use bear witness.[18] As with attitudes towards work, therefore, attitudes towards the punishment of children in care reflected attitudes towards the treatment of all children. Indeed, for much of its history, the care of separated children provides us with considerable insight into prevailing ideas about the status and upbringing of children in general.

That, however, may be changing. As social work develops, professional ideologies may well diverge from popular beliefs. Professional child care did not really appear until the first government-supported university training schemes were established as necessary accompaniments to the creation of local authority children's departments in 1948. Since then professional social work training has expanded and changed. New bodies of knowledge have been created with fashions of their own and with both explicit and implicit ideologies in train. It may be that, in child care, professional ideologies have come to replace those which were formerly derived from religion.

IV Reiteration

This introduction has done no more than indicate some of the major forces that have influenced the development of child care. All of them (and others as well) are discussed more fully in later chapters, each of which explores a particular strand of child care history. Other strands would have served equally well as points of departure and many are to be found interspersed throughout what follows. The object of the book is to show how child care history can be approached within its wider socio-economic setting and in a way that demonstrates both the persistence of some of the problems faced and the changes that have occurred in others. Similarly, it examines the way in which certain ideas about the appropriate solutions to those problems have remained remarkably consistent whilst others have changed radically over the years.

2 The age of separation

I The child rescuers

The Children Act of 1948 introduced the requirement that children in the care of local authorities should be restored to their parents wherever and as soon as possible. Until then it was common for the relationship between children in care and their parents to be effectively severed. This severance occurred both as a result of the pursuit of active policies to that end and as a result of inertia. Its active face owes its origin to the 19th century child-saving movement that was carried forward on the crest of the great wave of religious revivalism that swept through the second half of that century as well as to the growth of a legal structure which, under certain circumstances, provided that children could be removed from their parents and thereafter kept apart from them.

The child-saving movement

The core of the child-saving movement[1] is to be found in the many philanthropic organisations that proliferated in the 1860s and 1870s. The founders and leading figures of the largest of them – people like Barnardo, Müller, Stevenson and Waugh – became household names. Almost all were motivated by strong religious convictions and most of the organisations were denominational in character. Rivalry existed between them and, especially in the case of those associated with protestant evangelism, there was intense hostility towards the Catholic Church. The Catholic Church, in its turn, was deeply concerned about what it termed the 'leakage' from the faith and was especially sensitive to what it regarded as the proselytising activities of the protestant (and mostly evangelical) children's organisations. The development of the catholic children's societies was more often in the nature of a response to fears of protestant advancement and, with a few exceptions like Father Nugent of Liverpool,[2] less charismatic in its style.

Thus, one important feature of the child-saving movement was its sectarian rivalry and competition. A second feature, quite naturally, was that the 'saving' in question was essentially spiritual salvation. The work was typically regarded as a vocation. Convictions were deeply held throughout the organisations and, as mentioned in the introduction, they produced a determination and the kind of commitment that drove out doubt and uncertainty. Saving children was, therefore, an active mission in which the offspring of the poor were sought for their redemption and moral reclamation. However, this was not done without regard to their living conditions, for these were an indication of their spiritual need. Those conditions were of almost universal poverty – a poverty in which the well-being of the children was imperilled by the evils of crime, drunkenness, promiscuity, overcrowding, disease and begging. In order to be *saved*, children had to be *rescued* from the degradations that were distorting their lives as well as denying them spiritual salvation. The attraction of child-saving was that because children were seen as blameless and malleable they could be more readily reclaimed than adults. This being so, it was an effective means of forestalling the transmission of sinfulness into the next generation. Here, for example, is how Barnardo made the point:

> 'Reclamatory efforts among the adult population of our slums are heavily and often fatally handicapped by the gathered strength of years of bad habits, and of vicious indulgence; the *vis inertia* of ignorance, of vice, of crime, is only with difficulty overborne by the reforming forces brought to bear upon it. Hope, however, awakens when we cast our eyes upon *the Children*. Half our difficulties vanish when we have plastic material to work upon . . .'[3]

Even so, that work, it was believed, could not be accomplished without the creation of 'a new and healthy environment' of which 'a true and real religious life' was an indispensible part. The 'new environment' was at first almost wholly conceived in terms of the children's or rescue Home, although later it also took the form of boarding-out and emigration.

Locating the children to be 'saved'
How, then, did the emerging childrens societies of the second half of the 19th century go about saving children from the indisputably appalling conditions of Britain's slums? In terms of gathering in children there were essentially three processes:

- collection
- referral
- committal

The first of these corresponds most closely to the public image of the work of the societies that they themselves tended to cultivate. However, in the early years the many hungry, homeless and, to all intents and purposes, parentless children on the streets of the cities provided ample opportunity for 'collection'. Even so, it was necessary to have something practical to offer such children, and that was essentially food and shelter. There were many examples of night shelters, temporary refuges, free suppers or soup kitchens, but their drawback was that those whom they helped came and went and it was, therefore, impossible to exert any lasting influence upon their lives. What was needed, it seemed clear, were permanent arrangements whereby not only could children be fed, clothed and sheltered but also instructed, disciplined and brought within the reach of a steady Christian influence. The solution, again, was the residential Home.

Yet despite the widely publicised stories of forays into the night to locate and bring in children, as well as the accounts of children asking to be admitted, once the Homes had become established the flow of entrants became increasingly determined by systems of referral. These were of four kinds:

- those that originated with individual supporters around the country;
- those that were made by other organisations;
- those initiated by parents themselves; and
- those that arose from the decisions of the courts.

Referral by local branches and individual supporters
In the children's organisations that were linked to a diocesan system, such as the Catholic agencies and the Church of England Waifs and Strays Society, some referrals came from local branches. This, at least in the case of the Waifs and Strays, could be linked with arrangements for the referring person to sponsor the child in question financially. As one might imagine, such individualistic methods of referral led to a variety of interpretations of the circumstances under which a child needed to be taken into the care of the organisation. Central offices often became involved in arguments with local people or local branches about the particular merits of this or that case.

However, it was not only the diocesan-based societies that received referrals from the localities. All the societies developed schemes of subscribing members in order to encourage charitable donations. Many of these members, most of whom were ladies, took an active interest in the work and, from time to time, engaged in child rescue themselves – the results of which often led to a referral to the central body. This helps to explain why not all of the children in the care of the voluntary bodies came from the city slums. They also came from the country areas and spa towns, like Bath and Cheltenham, where the local branches or membership of the societies was likely to be strong.

Referral by other organisations

A second source of referral was, increasingly, from other welfare agencies of one kind or another, amongst which the often unacknowledged Poor Law was of considerable significance. All the societies looked with disfavour upon the Poor Law, seeing it as doing little more than perpetuating pauperism. Indeed, the view was frequently expressed that children not only needed to be saved from the evils of their environment but also from those associated with the Poor Law. In the case of the Catholic agencies this was a doubly important mission for, even after the interventions of central government in the 1870s that obliged guardians to keep creed registers and allow the Catholic inmates of their institutions to be visited by, and receive religious instruction from, a Catholic priest, many local boards of guardians remained hostile to Catholicism. The Catholic Church, in its turn, continued to be concerned about preserving the faith of Catholic children in what it saw as either the unduly secular or blatantly Protestant atmosphere of poor law schools and Homes. Catholic agencies began to invite guardians to transfer Catholic children to their care and succeeded in doing so by, amongst other things, reducing the fees that they charged to a level which cost-conscious guardians found attractive. By the latter part of the 19th century some three-quarters of the children in the care of the principal Catholic societies were poor law children being paid for by local boards of guardians.[4]

It was not the Catholic agencies alone, however, that received children from the Poor Law, although it is difficult to discover exactly how many were transferred because of the failure of the records to differentiate such children from the rest of those in the care of the voluntary societies. The Methodist National Children's Home appears to have received relatively few, whilst the Waifs and Strays admitted a steadily increasing proportion. For instance, its annual report for 1898 recorded that there was:

> 'an increasing disposition on the part of the Poor Law guardians to avail themselves of voluntary homes certified by the Local Government Board . . . about 150 Boards of Guardians have placed children in the Society's Homes, and by doing so have practically depauperised them although technically they remain paupers . . .'[5]

By 1901 the Society had 24 certified Homes providing 629 places. If all or most of these places had been allocated to poor law children they would have constituted about a fifth of the total number of children looked after by the Waifs and Strays. Of course, the picture was complicated

THE AGE OF SEPARATION

by the fact that, as we shall see, some societies ran reformatory and industrial schools to which a number of poor law children were sent; whilst others, like Barnardo's, did not. Nevertheless, some indication of the scale upon which poor law children were received into the care of the voluntary societies is provided by the number of their Homes which were certified by central government for this purpose. There were 266 in 1920 and 240 in 1934, but in the 1920s the Ministry of Health regularly reported that many boards of guardians were exceeding their powers by placing children in uncertified voluntary Homes.[6] In 1946 the Curtis Committee recorded that, altogether, somewhat over 4,500 poor law children were looked after in voluntary Homes of various kinds, or about 16 per cent of all those in such establishments.[7]

There were numerous reasons why boards of guardians should refer children in their care to voluntary societies. In some cases it was considered to be a cheaper alternative than, say, the construction of new children's Homes when numbers increased. In other instances it was because the voluntary societies had developed special services for the handicapped, sick or disabled children which many of the boards of guardians, having much smaller catchment areas, found it uneconomical to provide. Another reason for poor law referrals was to be found in the desire of some boards of guardians to take steps to ensure that their long-term charges did not become so accustomed to poor law provision that, as young adults and parents themselves, they turned automatically to the poor law for assistance in adversity. Finally, those boards of guardians who wished to emigrate some of the children in their Homes had no organisational means of doing so (having no relevant experience and no presence in Canada or Australia) and were, therefore, obliged to pass such children across to the voluntary societies, most of which had, by the 1890s, established systems for child emigration. Indeed some, like the Middlemore Homes in Birmingham, were almost wholly emigration societies. As a result of these transfers a large minority of the children who were emigrated to Canada between 1870 and the First World War as, for example, 'Barnardo boys and girls', would have been sent by and paid for by local boards of guardians.

It was not only the Poor Law however, that referred children to the voluntary societies. With the extension of its work from the 1890s onwards, the National Society for the Prevention of Cruelty to Children, which never established a long-term care system of its own, turned to other voluntary organisations when it became necessary to provide for a child away from its parents. Likewise, after the establishment of a probation system in 1907, probation officers sometimes used the

voluntary Homes, especially those admitting older children, when it
seemed impossible to supervise the youngsters in their charge in any other
way.[8]

Thus, the early practice and abiding image of societies engaged in the
direct rescue of children from the streets and low lodging houses was
soon replaced in reality by complicated networks of referrals that make
it difficult to know exactly how children came to be in the care of the
voluntary agencies, upon whose initiative, and with what financial implications. There is, in particular, the question of the extent to which parents
themselves sought the admission of their children and for what reasons.
That history is less well documented, although it is of considerable
importance, not least as a counter-balance to the image of the rescue
of abandoned, parentless or foresaken children.

Parental circumstances and family referrals
The issue touches closely upon the circumstances of mothers, and
especially upon the poverty of lone mothers, whether they were widows,
deserted or unmarried. Their treatment (or expected treatment) by the
Poor Law did much to determine their attitude towards the charitable
societies.[9] For example, whereas widowed mothers were likely to be
granted outdoor relief, it was less likely to be accorded to deserted wives
and much less so to unmarried mothers. If they were to provide for
themselves and their children they had to find paid work; but much of
the work that was available to them was in residential domestic service
or related occupations where children were not welcome. Lone mothers
who took such employment had to arrange for their children to be looked
after on a full-time basis. That ruled out the daily child-minding that was
available in most working-class areas. The admission of their children
to the care of a voluntary society provided an answer.

For these and other reasons, an uncounted number of mothers (and
some fathers and relatives too) applied to have their children admitted
to the care of the voluntary societies. Most, one imagines, did so with
sadness and regret, regarding it as the best of a limited number of
unpalatable options, and usually in the hope that the separation would
not be permanent, and that when things improved they could have their
children back.

Nonetheless, it is evident from the records and reports of many of the
societies that not every such application was successful – nor, indeed,
were applications from other sources. For instance, in 1890 Barnardo's
received nearly 6,400 requests for admission to care but accepted only
1,500 – or about a quarter.[10] The proportion of admissions to applications

was largest at the turn of the century when the Society took in every third referral.[11] Admission rates were higher in some other organisations. For instance, in 1904 the Waifs and Strays was accepting about 70 per cent of its 'formal' applications, although exactly how many 'informal' applications were steered away earlier in the procedures is unclear.[12] One suspects, although it is impossible to confirm, that many of the rejected applications in all the societies came from parents, for there was a clear view, expressed in many of the annual reports, that only the children of 'deserving' parents should be admitted. Several organisations declined to take illegitimate children, or at least refused them during part of their history. Others refused to accept a second or third illegitimate child from the same mother. A moral scrutiny was imposed, not least in order to avoid the charge that the societies were allowing parents to abdicate their responsibilities or, in the case of unmarried mothers, that they were encouraging promiscuity. That might also explain why many of the children who were admitted were described as orphans when they were not, although it needs to be borne in mind that the description 'orphaned in one parent' was often used. Orphanhood provided a moral justification for admission, as did waifdom or abandonment.

Referrals arising from decisions of the courts

Since the reformatory and industrial schools legislation of the 1850s, as we shall see in more detail in the next chapter, it had also been possible for courts to send children who had offended, or were in danger of doing so, to such schools and for them to be detained there until they had reached the ages of 18 or 16 respectively. At the start of this branch of the child-saving movement all these schools were run by voluntary bodies. They sometimes, therefore, received children through the mediation of the courts, although children were brought to the courts in the first place by diverse individuals and organisations as well as by their parents.

However, another landmark in the intervention of the courts in directing children to the voluntary societies occurred in 1889 with the passing of the Prevention of Cruelty to, and Protection of Children Act. Until then it had only been possible to proceed against parents who abused or ill-treated their children in very limited ways – the home, and what went on within it, remained an essentially private domain. Now, not only could cruel parents be charged, and if found guilty, punished, but the courts could order the removal of the children from their custody and place them in the care of a relative or a 'fit person' until, in the case of girls, they reached 16 or, if they were boys, 14.[13] The Act, and the mobilisation of the political support that secured its passage through Parliament, owed much to the tireless lobbying of Waugh and those around him in the newly-formed National Society for the Prevention of Cruelty to Children. However, the legislation was not unrelated to other important social changes that were occurring in the 1880s, especially those which were associated with the improvement of the legal status of women, and married women in particular. Until that time, with the barest of exceptions, fathers' rights over their children had reigned supreme. However, in 1878 the Matrimonial Causes Act had allowed justices to award the custody of their children to mothers in certain circumstances and, in 1886, the Guardianship of Infants Act enlarged mothers' rights to custody by providing that if the father died she became the legal guardian of her children. Under the Act she could also appoint guardians to assume the custody of her children after her death, and she could apply to the court to make any order it saw fit regarding custody and access but having 'regard to the welfare of the child', the conduct of the parents and the wishes of either parent. Thus, at last, in Pinchbeck and Hewitt's words, 'the courts in England were given full jurisdiction to override completely the old common law rights of the father in relation to the custody of his infant children'.[14] However, it was not until 1925 that full legal equality of the parents in respect to the guardianship of their children was achieved.[15]

Of course, few if any of these changes affected the lives of the poor. But they were indications of a gradual change in the position of women although, of course, women were not successful in winning the right to vote until 1919 and many social, legal and political disqualifications persisted thereafter. Nonetheless, by the 1880s progress had been made and this is politically important in the history of child care; for the fortunes of children and women were, and continue to be, closely interwoven. Both the Prevention of Cruelty to Children Act of 1889, and the Poor Law (Amendment) Act that reached the statute book in the same year and enabled boards of guardians to assume parental rights over children in their care in certain circumstances, were passed against a background in which the rights of fathers over their children were no longer paramount and in which certain rights were beginning to be accorded to women. The protection of the rights of children against abuse by their parents could be more readily established from such a foundation.

The importance of the 1889 Prevention of Cruelty legislation to the question of how children reached the voluntary children's societies lay in the provision that justices could now commit abused children to the care of a relative or a 'fit person'. Sometimes there was a relative who was considered to be suitable; more often there was not. Increasingly, therefore, children were committed to the care of organisations such as the NSPCC, Barnardo's, the Waifs and Strays and so on, although those like the NSPCC who had little or no care facilities of their own then made arrangements with other societies to look after the children who had been placed in their care. However, since no financial provision was made to meet the costs of the 'fit person', the societies quickly began to apply to the courts for maintenance orders against the parents, even though it was frequently difficult to extract the payments.

After 1889, the effect of the legislation was to ensure a small but steady flow of children from the courts to a relatively small number of voluntary organisations. However, since the children remained in their custody until they were 16 (boys were put on a par with girls in 1894) the number rapidly accumulated. Practically, of course, the actual legal status of these children was not easily distinguished once they had been absorbed into organisations such as Barnardo's. Furthermore, since there was much concern about the dangers of these children returning to their parents when the orders expired, a large proportion of them, particularly in the first 20 years after the legislation, were emigrated to Canada. Between 1899 and 1909, for example, at least 800 such children crossed the Atlantic, 500 being sent by Barnardo's alone.[16]

The grounds upon which custody orders to fit persons could be made were gradually extended. In the 1908 Children Act, for instance, it was laid down for the first time that neglect could include a failure to provide adequate food, clothing, medical aid or lodging. Justices were also enabled to make a fit person order instead of an industrial school order when children were, for example, found begging, wandering, living in brothels or offending when they were under 12. After the 1933 Children and Young Persons Act, fit person orders could be made in respect of certain juvenile offenders, but by then courts were mainly making the committals to the local authorities, not to the voluntary societies.

The commitment of voluntary societies to expansion

We have noted that none of the organisations was able or prepared to admit all the children for whom they received applications. Nonetheless, for at least three reasons, all were keen to accept as many 'appropriate' cases as possible. First, for economic reasons it was essential to keep the available 'places' fully utilised, especially as the income from the fees provided by the public sector became increasingly important. Secondly, in order to sustain and stimulate charitable donations it was necessary to be seen to be active and successful. Growth was a valuable index, and the most important expansion was in the number of children who were saved by being admitted to care. There was a third, extremely important, reason why the voluntary societies were committed to expansion – the sectarian rivalry which has already been mentioned. Evidence of organisational competition was present from the outset.

There were, therefore, strongly-rooted factors – religious, economic and organisational – that tended to encourage rather than to discourage the admission of children to the care of the voluntary societies. Furthermore, because of their keen desire to retain children as a protective and preventive measure, numbers inevitably grew. There was the constant dilemma, therefore, of how, under these circumstances, the newcomers were to be accommodated; and the newcomers were vitally important to the public image of active and effective child saving. One answer was further capital development to provide extra Homes, but expansion of this kind was hazardous since all the organisations faced periods of financial crisis. A major alternative was emigration. It appealed to the child-saving motive, conveying as it did the sense of a new start in an environment of rural uprightness, out of reach of the evils of either the slums or wanton and irresponsible parents. At the same time, it helped to solve the problem of how to maintain or increase the number of admissions. In Barnardo's words (and others echoed his sentiments):

> 'A rescue Home must . . . be continuously gathering in fresh inmates, else it would in a single generation be compelled to give the signal of retreat and close its doors, and write up in the face of new applicants: 'no admission'. But to secure *the open door in front* it must maintain its *exit door* in the rear (original emphasis)'.[17]

Child emigration, which reached its peak in the early years of the 20th century, enlarged the size of the door at the rear considerably, as, to some extent, did the development of boarding-out. Of course, another solution would have been to have discharged children sooner and restored them to their parents, but that was rarely done because of the dominant belief in the value of severance. Indeed, as noted at the beginning of this chapter, the long period of child care history up to the 1948 Children Act was characterised as one of 'severance'. However, this period can be divided into two phases: the first, during which there was deliberate severance and a later one, in which the severance that occurred did so more often as the result of inertia. Let us examine each phase in turn.

II Active severance

We have seen that, as time passed, children came into the care of the voluntary children's societies via numerous routes and for an assortment of reasons. However, once in care, policies were pursued in order to keep some children apart from what were regarded as the contaminating influences of their parents. In practice these policies spilled over to affect most children. Whatever the actual reason for a child being admitted to care, it became common for the societies to behave as if all were the victims of worthless, untrustworthy or incompetent parents. This was partly a reflection of the strong emphasis that was placed upon the idea of child rescue and partly a reflection of the contemporary unwillingness to acknowledge the structural forces in society that made it exceedingly difficult for some parents, especially lone mothers or those with large families, to bring up their children in an adequate fashion. This, in its turn, was linked to the grave suspicion with which, paradoxically, all the charitable societies regarded charitable giving in the form of financial assistance, especially any form of regular payment comparable with poor law relief. Such handouts, it was widely believed, simply made matters worse, plunging the recipients even more deeply into the slough of dependence from which they became less and less able – or willing – to escape by their own efforts.

However, there was a profound contradiction in the application of these attitudes and beliefs to the work of the child-saving societies for, as we have seen, at the point of admission they did differentiate between deserving and undeserving parents, at least when it came to deciding about the applications they received from parents. If some parents were deserving, that is if some of them were the unfortunate victims of circum- stances beyond their control, then they could hardly be classed together with those who were dangerous or evil and from whom it was crucial to keep children apart. There was no good reason not to return children to deserving parents if and when their circumstances improved or, indeed, to help such parents to be able to have their children back. Yet, for at least three reasons, this was rarely done.

Some reasons why children rarely returned to their parents
One of these reasons lay in the patterns of material adversity and improvement that parents experienced. The times of most severe difficulty were when children were young and entirely dependent. There was, however, a brief period in which poor families could expect to be somewhat better-off – a period before their offspring left home, but after

they had reached an age when they could earn money and supplement the family income. However, when parents sought to have their children back as they reached these useful ages their motives were treated with deep suspicion. They *only* wanted their children back now, so it was repeatedly asserted, for what they could earn. By asking to have them back when they could afford to do so, even those parents who were at first numbered amongst the deserving became classed as exploitative, grasping and unworthy. The irony, of course, was that many of the Homes, as well as the reformatory and industrial schools, argued that the older children could not be released early, or sent out to full-time education, because the work that they did in an institution was so crucial to its economy. Even by 1925, for example, it was reported that when they pressed voluntary Homes to send their children to the local schools, Home Office inspectors were told more than once that this was not possible because 'we should never get the housework done'.[18]

Another reason why even 'deserving' parents frequently found it difficult to recover their children was connected with the duration of their stay. The longer children stayed in the care of the societies, the more likely it became that parents would be dismissed as indifferent, uncaring or irresponsible. They had, or so it seemed, virtually abandoned their children in care. This view was often reinforced if the parents failed to make the regular financial contributions that they were asked to pay. Of course, some parents *did* consciously abandon their children to the care of the societies, but many others were deterred from maintaining links by the policies of severance that tended to be applied irrespective of the fitness of the parents.

Limitations upon parental visiting

The policies of severance took various forms but two in particular provide ample illustration. First, there were the severe limitations that were placed upon visiting and other forms of communication. Home visits were rarely allowed and, in many cases, rules were laid down about how often parents could visit their child and at what time. It was not unusual for parents to be restricted to one visit every three months and for limitations also to be placed upon the number of letters that a child could receive or send. In some cases these rules (which did not, of course, have the force of law) were set out in the agreement forms that parents applying for the reception of their children were required to sign.

Severance by distance

The barrier of distance constituted a second group of policies that aimed at achieving severance. The fact that many of the large voluntary societies took children from all over the country incidentally served that purpose. Boarding-out in the countryside, well away from the towns, had the same effect. However, the most explicit and effective means of keeping children from their parents was through emigration. The value of emigration was frequently emphasised as a method of finally removing children from *all* parental influence. Some of the societies used agreement forms that included a paragraph which said that, if it was thought necessary, a child could be emigrated; and this operated as one of the conditions for admission. Parents often signed the forms over a postage stamp and this must have persuaded many of them that the conditions were legally binding and inescapable. Of course, they were not – as from time to time the societies were advised by solicitors whose opinions they sought. Some, like the Waifs and Strays, dropped the clause from their document early on, but others, like Barnardo's, retained it into the 20th century. Most of the emigrated children were sent to Canada and many went without the explicit agreement – and sometimes without the knowledge – of their parents or relatives.[19] Given the poverty of virtually all the parents, even a journey across London or Liverpool to the suburbs presented a daunting prospect. A visit to a child who was boarded-out in a more distant rural community posed an even greater problem, whilst the likelihood of parents ever being able to cross the Atlantic was as remote as a trip to the moon.

Thus, there was a variety of policies and practices that reflected the conviction that, for their own good, the ties with their parents of many children in care should be severed or, at least, weakened.

Legal backing for the policies of severance

Largely at the instigation of the child rescue movement, this philosophy of severance was strengthened at the beginning of the 1890s by new laws that gave the societies greater power to retain children in their care. Two important pieces of legislation reached the statute book in 1891. First there was the Custody of Children Act, and then the Reformatory and Industrial Schools Act.

The Custody of Children Act followed, in large part, from the major Barnardo court cases that began in 1889. The issue involved three children in Barnardo's care – Harry Gossage, Martha Tye and John Roddy – whose parents sought to have their children returned to them. As Wagner explains, 'two were immediately bundled out of the country in such a way that they could not be traced, and Barnardo applied to the courts to support his claim for the custody of John James Roddy'.[20] In each case, however, 'he was fighting to retain custody not principally to prevent children returning to cruel and neglectful parents, but to prevent their being brought up as Roman Catholics'.[21] The protracted litigation attracted considerable public attention and brought into sharp relief both the question of the rights of parents as opposed to the welfare of their children and also the willingness of Barnardo in particular (although there were also others) to adopt subterfuge, deception, and illegal methods in order to prevent children from being returned to parents who, for one reason or another, were considered to be unfit. In these particular cases, however, a further complication was added because the intention of the parents was not to look after the children themselves, but to have them brought up in Catholic Homes.

The Custody of Children Act, 1891
The cases provided a vivid example of the unsatisfactory nature of the law of custody of children. There was no legal means whereby children who had been admitted to the care of a voluntary society (unless committed by a court under the fit person order procedure or having been made the subject of a reformatory or industrial school order) could be kept against the wishes of their parents, some of whom were undoubtedly unfit to have custody of them. As Wagner concludes, the outcome of the litigation was partly a defeat and partly a victory for Barnardo.[22] He was defeated in that the writs of *habeas corpus* were upheld by the House of Lords (although, in fact, the children were never located, so they were not returned). However, he won a longer-term victory in that it became increasingly evident that if the rights of children were to be protected adequately, then the law of custody had to be revised. This was the background, therefore, against which, on a third attempt, a bill was successfully introduced in Parliament, to become the Custody of Children Act, 1891.

If parents could be shown to have abandoned or deserted their child, or have conducted themselves in a way that the court considered made them unfit to have custody, then their application for a writ or order for the production of the child could be refused. Furthermore, under the new law any person or institution could acquire the right of custody in place of parents who could not pay the costs that had been incurred in looking after their child. Obviously, that clause made it extremely difficult for poor parents to recover their children – leaving aside the question of their fitness to do so. Allowing one's child to be in someone else's care and being unable or unwilling to meet the expense was, therefore, interpreted as a form of abandonment. This legislation, therefore considerably strengthened the hands of the voluntary children's societies in their determination to prevent parents whom they regarded as vicious, irresponsible or immoral from having their children back.

The Reformatory and Industrial Schools Act, 1891

The 1891 Custody of Children Act was only the first of two pieces of legislation passed that year which contributed to that end: the other was the Reformatory and Industrial Schools Act. The purpose of that Act, it was explained in Parliament, was 'to abolish the right of parents of children in Industrial and Reformatory Schools, where they have been educated for a time, to have these children home again at the end of the period of detention'. It did not stop children going home if they wished to do so. Its object was 'to prevent parents compelling children, against their wish, to go back to a home where, possibly, they will be taught extremely bad habits and be placed in circumstances which will lead to their relapsing into crime'.[23] The means by which these provisions could be achieved were through directing girls into residential domestic service, encouraging boys to enlist or, for both girls and boys, arranging their emigration. Hitherto, both enlistment and emigration had required parental permission.

Obviously the impetus behind this legislation was similar to that which gave rise to the Custody of Children Act and it reflected the same groundswell of political support for child protection. In this case, however, the pressure group contained a much wider spectrum of interests which, as well as the main children's societies included, for example, the Girls' Friendly Society, the Central Poor Law Conference and those, of course, who represented the reformatory and industrial schools. What the lobbyists originally wanted were powers to retain children in the industrial school system until they were 18 rather than 16 (they could already be held until they were 18 in reformatories) if it could be shown before magistrates that the restoration of parental control would 'prejudice' a child's future. This they wanted linked to a scheme for licensing that extended beyond the full term of the order, with provision for recall. What the Act eventually gave them was much watered down, largely as a result of Home Office unease. The schools were able to dispense with parental permission for apprenticeship, enlistment or emigration, but only if the child agreed and, equally important, only with the approval of the Home Secretary in each case.

Despite its severely truncated form, the 1891 Reformatory and Industrial Schools Act was one of the fruits of a distinctive campaign to reduce parental rights in the cause of child protection that had been active and influential since the mid-1880s. One of its most fascinating features was the interconnections within and between the groups of evangelists, social reformers and philanthropists who banded together for this purpose. What was equally interesting was the considerable caution with which the senior civil servants at the Home Office (almost all of whom were lawyers) treated encroachments upon parental rights in favour of the voluntary societies.

Boards of guardians and severance policies

Thus far we have discussed the child-saving movement as if it existed entirely within the voluntary sector and certainly this was the source of the most vigorous and sustained initiatives. The position of boards of guardians was, however, more complex and certainly more unpredictable, there being over 600 of them throughout England and Wales until the local government reforms of 1930. There was, of course, a keen desire on the part of guardians as well as the central board to keep expenditure on poor relief to a minimum. It was not surprising, therefore, that various steps were taken to encourage parents to resume the care of children who had been admitted for 'indoor relief'. For example, despite the fact that when parents and children were admitted together the children (unless they were young babies) were separated from their parents, these same parents were not permitted to leave the workhouse unless they took their children with them. Some guardians also threatened that unless the care of a child in their care was taken over by parents or a relative, he or she would be boarded-out in some distant locality or, indeed, emigrated. In some areas during the 1870s and 80s, notices to this effect were displayed in prominent places – listing the children proposed for such disposals.

Of course, the whole thrust of the poor law policy was to deter people from applying for help. In that respect it was quite unlike the voluntary societies, whose general attitude was to welcome the opportunity of rescuing imperilled children by taking them into their care. However, this distinction is too simple. We have seen already that the charitable societies took in far fewer children than were referred to them. Likewise, the boards of guardians had at least one good reason for admitting poor children: their wish to reduce the cost of *all* forms of relief and not simply the cost of providing relief in their institutions. In terms of current expenditure at least, out-door relief was the expensive and difficult to control aspect of their activities. As we have seen, one way of reducing that cost was to take in some of the children of lone mothers so that the women could obtain work. Thus, the quest for economy actually led some guardians, especially in the urban areas, actively to offer to receive some children in a family, in order to avoid admitting them all.

Whereas most of the children who came into the care of the voluntary societies were accepted, either explicitly or implicitly, on a long-term basis, the boards of guardians had to deal with what were termed the 'ins' and outs'. These were the children of destitute or homeless families who, living from one short-term crisis to the next, returned time after time for a short period of relief before discharging themselves once more. Again, however, there was an underlying contradiction which posed a dilemma for the guardians. On the one hand, the quick discharge of a family removed them from the relief rolls but, on the other, their children were not in the institutions long enough to be properly absorbed into the poor law school system which was regarded as the principal agent in breaking the cycle of pauperism. The 'ins and outs' were, therefore, considered to be in danger of becoming a perpetual pauper class because their children could not be brought under the control and training that was necessary to wean them from lives of pauper dependence. This was one reason why some boards of guardians pressed to have stronger powers to retain children. Another, and more important, was the concern that many entertained about allowing children to return to cruel and, especially, sexually abusive parents. As it was, there was nothing they could do to prevent parents (and especially fathers) from taking their children back.

The Poor Law (Amendment) Act, 1889
This situation changed in 1889, with the passing of the Poor Law (Amendment) Act. Its key feature was the first section (often described as poor law adoption) which ran as follows:

> 'Where a child is maintained by the guardians of any union and was deserted by its parent, the guardians may at any time resolve that such a child shall be under the control of the guardians until it reaches the age, if a boy, 16, and if a girl, 18 years, and thereupon until the child reaches that age all powers and rights of such parent in respect of that child shall . . . rest in the guardians.'

During its progress through Parliament it was explained that an amendment act of this kind was necessary because there was 'no sufficient or adequate protection for the interests of the children against being handed over to the care of their relatives or guardians if those relatives or guardians are obviously unfit to take charge of them'. However, it was added that there was 'no likelihood of the guardians being unduly anxious to maintain

the children at the expenses of the rates if those who would otherwise
have to maintain them are of a sufficient character to discharge that
duty'.[24]

This poor law legislation was, of course, swept forward by the same
tide that carried with it the other important child care legislation of the
period 1889-91. However, in this case the pressure had been exerted
upon a reluctant central Local Government Board by local boards of
guardians. For instance, in 1887 a delegation from the Manchester Poor
Law Conference met the president of the LGB to impress upon him
the need for them to be able to retain children if their well-being was
endangered by allowing them to return to their parents. This, as well
as the impact of other poor law delegations and memoranda arguing for
similar reforms, was doubtless one of the reasons why the Lords' Select
Committee on Poor Law Relief (which was set up for rather different
purposes) considered the matter so fully in 1888.[25]

Changing attitudes and legal powers of boards of guardians
The point to be made, of course, is that the distinction that tends to
be drawn between the benevolent concern for children of the philanthropic
bodies and the hard-faced indifference of boards of guardians is too crude
and over-generalised. By the 1880s women and representatives of labour
were beginning to be elected as guardians, and it had always been common
to find clergymen amongst the board members. Boards of guardians were
not homogeneous, neither in the views of their membership (as many
close votes on child care issues attest) nor from one board to another.
Many were just as concerned about the welfare of the children in their
care as the charitable societies although, of course, they had a much wider
range of responsibilities and were not influenced as powerfully by the
ideology of child saving.

So, from 1889 onwards the guardians were able to take steps to prevent
parents from resuming the care of their children. However, these new
powers were strengthened further by the 1891 Custody of Children Act
which we have discussed already in relation to the voluntary societies.
In particular, it limited more severely a court's power to reverse a
resolution made by a board of guardians. Previously, a parent's complaint
would prevail if it could be shown that the child had not been maintained
by the guardians or, more especially, that the child had not been deserted,
or that the order should be set aside in the interest of the child's welfare.
From 1891, the onus was placed upon the parent to prove himself or
herself a fit person. Furthermore, the Act provided that if the court did

order the child to be given up, the parents had to pay to the guardians 'the whole of the costs properly incurred in bringing up the child'.

By 1949 the proportion of children in the care of local authorities who were subject to what became known as 'parental rights resolutions' stood at 14 per cent. Of all those who could have been made subject to such a resolution (that is, the total in care less those committed on fit person orders) the proportion was about 19 per cent.[26] 'Poor Law adoption' had become, therefore, a significant practice by the time that the new children's departments were set up in 1948. It has continued to be operated very much along the lines that were first introduced in 1889, although the new child care legislation that is currently proposed would oblige local authorities to refer proposals for the assumption of parental rights to a court of law.[27]

Changes in the legal framework protecting children from their parents

The legal framework which secured the rights of children to be protected from their parents was established by the beginning of the 1890s, although it was mainly expressed in terms of the circumstances in which welfare organisations could assume the rights formerly invested in the parents. As the years passed, various additions and modifications were made (with a major consolidation in the 1908 Children Act) but the principles remained virtually unchanged until the Children Act of 1975. One important exception was the Adoption of Children Act, 1926 which introduced adoption into English law for the first time, although the practice and the terminology had existed long before.[28]

III Inertia

At the beginning of this chapter we suggested that the principle of severance that dominated the policy and practice of child care had first been actively implemented and later simply allowed to continue. This second aspect was as important in maintaining the *reality* of severance as the first and can be related especially to the inter-war years. There was less close adherence to the 'principle' of severance but no great initiatives were taken to modify or replace it. Several factors combined to produce that state of affairs.

The 1914-18 War and its effects on child care organisations

The war of 1914-18 had caused considerable organisational disruption in child care, especially as a result of the conscription that was introduced in 1916. Younger staff were lost, some as casualties, whilst others chose not to return to their pre-war posts. Women as well as men were affected. Most of the societies and local government operated under considerable pressure during the war and took time to return to a peace-time footing. The number of children in the care of both the Poor Law and voluntary societies reached a peak in 1917 but began to decline after the war had ended. These upheavals might have provided the opportunity for a radical reassessment of child care policies and practices but, for several reasons, whatever opportunities there were passed without being taken.

By the 1920s the children's societies had moved away from their early phase in which charismatic leadership and enthusiastic evangelism provided powerful motive forces. Barnardo had died in 1905, Waugh in 1908 and Stevenson in 1912. Rudolf lived on until 1933 but was succeeded as the secretary of the Waifs and Strays Society in 1919. In Stroud's words, 'all the captains and kings had departed'.[29] Secondly, the war had challenged accepted values and beliefs. One consequence was a growing secularism. In particular, 19th century style revivalism was a spent force. The societies had 'matured' into formal organisations, and furthermore, most of them were facing financial problems. Charitable giving had withered with the decline of religious zeal and the imposition of the high rates of personal income tax that had been necessary to pay for the war. The societies became preoccupied with the state of their accounts, in which income from public bodies, by way of fees and grants, tended to play a lesser part than it had done during the war years.

These financial stringencies affected the small organisations especially, for although it is tempting to treat the history of voluntary child care as if it were the history of the half-dozen or so large nationally organised societies, there were, throughout the 19th century and well into the 20th, hundreds of Homes and orphanages run by religious communities, employers, local benefactors or small informal committees. Until the 1933 Children and Young Persons Act imposed registration, there was no record of the number of such institutions or anything about the children whom they accommodated. Before then they were not required to notify anyone of their existence unless they wished to take poor law children or operate as reformatory or industrial schools. There was, therefore, no general system for their inspection. Between 1933 and 1938 about 1,000 such Homes notified their existence to the Home Office as required but there were certainly many others that failed to do so. As late as 1938 the Home Office could report that it knew of 'small homes of 10, 20 or 30 children whose committees and heads, absorbed in their good work, reading only a local or religious newspaper, hear nothing of recent legislation'.[30] When first inspected, the conditions in many of the Homes were found to be unsatisfactory and the inspectors described some as 'appalling'.

If there were 1,250 taking on average 20 children, then there would have been some 25,000 children in these Homes. That would mean that the total number of children in the care of the voluntary societies could have been underestimated by that figure – or the equivalent in 1939 of another three organisations the size of Barnardo's. The history of most of these small local children's Homes, orphanages or refuges remains obscure. Little is known of how they came to be established, how they were run, what the experiences of the children who lived in them were, or why and when they closed their doors.

Voluntary societies during the inter-war years

Unlike the Poor Law and the reformatory and industrial schools, the number of children in the care of the main voluntary societies did not fall in the inter-war years; indeed, from the early 1920s the trend was slightly upwards. This owed a good deal to the greater length of time that children remained with them, for, at least until the Second World War, they provided mainly long-term care. Indeed, if the societies were to use their residential resources economically they could not afford to have too many vacancies and, in any case, as we have seen, there was no tradition of rehabilitating children with their families.

Even had this been adopted as a new policy the societies, with the exception of the NSPCC, had not built up a large enough body of field staff who could work to this end – and provide help and supervision afterwards, or even to keep contact with the families. Most of their staff were employed in residential Homes. Without far-reaching and costly changes the societies were unable to do anything that differed very much from what they had always done. Almost by default, therefore, the policies and practices of severance that had become so firmly rooted in the 19th century continued to dictate what happened in the 20th. This was the legacy and the tradition which, *faut de mieux*, continued to prevail. It is, indeed, difficult to discover very much that was novel in the work of the voluntary children's societies in the 20 years between the wars, although some, like the NCH, did introduce training schemes for residential staff. In general, however, they had become stultified: their heyday had passed and it was not until the 1970s that a renewed vigour became evident and new policies began to emerge.

Boards of guardians and the inter-war years

If little was changing in the voluntary sector in the inter-war years at least the number of children in the care of the boards of guardians, and their successors the local authority public assistance committees, fell sharply.

That apart, the reform of local government after 1930 implanted seeds
of change, mainly because the numerous boards of guardians disappeared
and their responsibilities were taken over by larger county councils and
county borough councils. Of course, size did not automatically lead to
more enlightened policies although some of the largest authorities, like
London County Council, had the resources and the imagination to introduce, support or expand a variety of forward-looking schemes such as
child guidance clinics, staff training and a home visiting service staffed
by volunteers.

Nevertheless the Poor Law, even in its new guise, did little to change
established policies and practices in terms of preserving links between
children in care and their parents. There was still a heavy reliance upon
residential care, and what field work there was was liable to be undertaken
by a mixture of officers scattered between different departments; for
example, relieving officers, health visitors or school attendance officers.
As in the voluntary sector, many children not only remained separated
from their parents but lost contact through a combination of factors. In
some cases authorities were content to see it happen, whilst in others
they failed to regard it as a problem or simply lacked the will or the
resources to do anything about it. The net result was much the same:
separation led to severance.

Post Second World War reform

It would be wrong to assume, however, that the blaze of reform after
the Second World War and the inclusion in the 1948 Children Act of
a requirement that local authorities should aim for the rehabilitation of
children in care with their parents, ended the age of severance. Despite
the new ideology, children continued to languish in care and discouraged
parents faded from the picture. This was rarely because these were the
ends sought by the new genre of child care officers but because other
priorities seemed more pressing, and because there was, after all, a deep-
rooted legacy of long-term child rescue to be superseded. Tradition, habit
and the pressure of other matters allowed children to 'wait in care' on
a scale and in ways described by Rowe and Lambert in 1973,[31] and for
their links with their families to be weakened or fractured in ways that
Millham and his colleagues were still able to record in 1986.[32]

We shall return to this theme in Chapter 5 in the context of the
development of policies for rehabilitation and prevention. For the
moment, however, it is necessary to return to the 19th century in order
to consider first what the history of the reformatory and industrial schools
and then of boarding-out can tell us about the factors that were important
in the emergence of particular forms of care for separated children.

3 Reformatory and industrial schools – an institutional solution

I Origins – the 19th century

The reformatory and industrial school systems were combined in 1933 to form a single category of approved schools which have subsequently become designated as community homes with education provided on the premises. Although private and voluntary reformatory and industrial schools had been established in various parts of the country from the end of the 18th century,[1] the period of most rapid expansion began in the 1850s and was marked by a Reformatory Schools Act in 1854, followed by an Industrial Schools Act in 1857. This legislation, as well as some subsequent amendments, was consolidated in a general Reformatory and Industrial Schools Act in 1866, and that remained the principal statute until the revisions that were introduced by the Children Act of 1908.

The legislation enabled the courts to send any child under 16 (a minimum age of 10 was subsequently introduced) to a reformatory but only after the expiry of a prison sentence. Such children could be kept in the reformatory from two to five years until they reached 18 (and later 19) years of age. The legislation also gave the courts authority to order that children up to the age of 14 be sent to an industrial school and retained there until they were 15 (and later until they were 16). The grounds upon which an industrial school order could be made were extensive and further additions were made as time passed. Mainly, however, the aim was to combat child vagrancy and begging, but those who were found wandering and destitute or who were known to frequent the company of thieves could also be committed to an industrial school by the courts. So too could children under 14 who were charged by their parents as being beyond their control. Later amendments provided for the children of criminal or drunken parents to be included as well as girls who lived in brothels or whose fathers had been found guilty of sexually assaulting them. Not least, of course, as we have seen, committal to an industrial school became the ultimate sanction against those children who failed to attend school once elementary education became compulsory.

Reformatories were for somewhat older children who had been convicted of an offence – indeed, their prior imprisonment was a precondition for admission until 1893 when it became optional. The industrial schools mainly took younger children who, in more modern terminology, might be regarded as being in need of care or protection. However, young offenders under the age of 12 could also be sent to an industrial school which, given that the age of criminal responsibility was then 7, could comprise a fairly large group.

These details indicate the categories of children for whom the reformatory and industrial school systems were intended. They also remind us of the extent to which successive legislation, right up to the present, has incorporated themes (and indeed some of the terminology) from the 1850s. However, in order to understand the significance of the reformatory and industrial schools in the history of child care and, more particularly, in the history of residential child care, three questions need to be considered:

- What problems were such institutions set up to solve?
- Why did they proliferate so rapidly in the 1850s and 1860s?
- What form did they take?

What problems did they address?
The answer to the first question is relatively simple and can be found repeated *ad nauseam* in the literature of the period.[2] Essentially the problem was conceived as a rising tide of juvenile disorder that manifested itself most clearly in juvenile crime but also in the twin problems of begging and vagrancy. In short, the children of the under-class had to be brought under control in order partly to protect society, but also in order to rescue them from sinful and wasted lives and especially from the contagion of repeated imprisonment. Since there appeared to be every indication that the problem was growing, steps also needed to be taken to prevent children from becoming hardened criminals and, more importantly, to prevent them from becoming the next generation of feckless, irresponsible or wantonly neglectful parents.

Why did they proliferate in the 1850s and '60s
These were not new concerns and, therefore, we must ask why the 1850s and 1860s witnessed such a marked surge of action. There are at least two answers. One is simply that the problem of the disorderly young was seen as more urgent, both because of its scale and because of its visibility. This was partly attributable to the rapid growth of urbanisation

but also to the changing character and level of demand for child labour. Technical developments in both industry and agriculture had begun to make certain kinds of child labour redundant, whilst the imposition of legal restrictions upon the terms and conditions under which they could work had also begun to make it less attractive to employ them. These changes were superimposed upon the much earlier growth of wage labour that had accompanied the development of industrialisation and especially the factory system. This had finally destroyed the domestic economies in which many children had once worked alongside their parents as a family unit. By the middle decades of the 19th century, widespread wage labour, technical change, the regulation of children's employment, and urbanisation had combined to create a class of children that was subject neither to the discipline of organised work nor to parental oversight, since many mothers and fathers were drawn away from the home into long hours of labour elsewhere.

However, these changes have to be seen in the context of two other circumstances. The first was the profound poverty in which many labouring families lived, a poverty enforced upon them both by low wages and by the casual and erratic patterns of employment that were intensified by an economy prone to periods of boom followed by periods of deep depression.[3] The plight of poor families became even more desperate if sickness or death left mothers as the sole breadwinners. Although widows commonly remarried, this was liable to increase the number of mouths to feed as families were augmented and dwellings overcrowded by an assortment of children from a variety of marriages. Left to their own devices, the children of the poor did what they could for themselves or for their families by begging, stealing, running errands, carrying bags, or holding horses. Some formed themselves into all-too-conspicuous gangs whose activities caused especial alarm.

The virtual absence of a school system exacerbated these economic changes which were redefining the position of the child in the middle years of the 19th century. The 1850s and '60s, therefore, were decades in which the collapse of earlier forms of control over poor children had yet to be replaced by a comprehensive and compulsory system of education. It was only after the 1870 Education Act that free, compulsory and (eventually) universal elementary education was gradually established.

What form did they take?
Against this background both the growth and the form of the reformatory and industrial schools became understandable. In the 1840s, in particular, there had been numerous philanthropic ventures to provide day schools,

Sunday schools, industrial residential schools and reformatories. Their weaknesses however (typified by the Ragged School Movement) were their lack of sufficient and reliable funds and their inability to compel attendance. In the case of the day schools, they were often only part-time or only took children on certain days of the week. The importance of the reformatory and industrial schools legislation of the 1850s was that it introduced legal compulsion through court procedures. Children who were found to be in certain circumstances could be obliged to enter institutions and could then be kept there for long periods – eventually, as we have seen, in the case of the reformatories until they were 19 and in the industrial schools until they were 16; and children as young as 5 or 6 could be sent to an industrial school.

Why were they run by voluntary bodies?
One further question remains. Why, despite a good deal of pressure for the reformatory and industrial schools to be run by public bodies, was their development mainly left in the hands of voluntary societies? There are several explanations. First, most of what had already been done had been the result of philanthropic initiative. Secondly, local government was weak and underdeveloped – the only existing local public agencies that might have run such institutions would have been the boards of guardians or, possibly, the county prison system. Neither was an attractive option. Local guardians had little enthusiasm for assuming additional responsibilities and, in any case, many of the philanthropists and others saw the purpose of these new institutions as protecting children from the pauperising effects of the Poor Law as well as preventing their contamination by the experience of prison. Thirdly, central government had neither the means nor the inclination to become directly involved in the administration of these establishments. The Privy Council on Education had virtually no funds, the Poor Law Board was weak and operated almost entirely through local boards of guardians, whilst the Home Office was preoccupied with such matters as a prison system in chaos and a still newly-established series of police forces around the country.

Nonetheless, the legislation did empower the Treasury to give financial support which, mainly in the form of *per capita* grants, facilitated the rapid growth of first the reformatories and then the industrial schools in the second half of the 1850s and in the 1860s. The supply of children who attracted these grants was ensured by the new element of compulsion.

The growth of industrial schools
After a pronounced surge at the beginning the numbers in reformatories soon reached a plateau in the middle years of the 1870s. By contrast,

the industrial schools went from strength to strength to accommodate a peak population of over 19,400 in Great Britain in 1898, of whom about 1,750 were on licence. Why, therefore, was there such a dramatic increase in the number of children in industrial schools? One reason was the lack of a sufficient diversity in the range of disposals available to magistrates. Many children might not have been committed to industrial schools (or reformatories for that matter) had lesser penalties been available or had there been an effective means of fining parents.

Another reason for the rise in the numbers in industrial schools as opposed to reformatories was, as we have seen, the remarkable range of grounds upon which a child could be brought before the justices. Furthermore, since children were not charged with a criminal offence the rules of evidence were less stringent than when they were and this both encouraged and enabled a variety of people to present children to the courts as in need of the protection or discipline that an industrial school was assumed to offer. Home visitors, Bible women, relieving officers, or indeed anyone else who chose to concern themselves with a child's condition, could bring them before a court.

However, in 1876 the Elementary Education Act made the newly-constituted school boards the responsible authorities for the local administration of the Industrial Schools Act. They were charged with seeing that children who required to be sent to such schools were so committed. Whereas formerly it was nobody's business in particular to take the initiative in directing children towards the industrial schools, it now became the responsibility of the local authority. It remained possible for anybody else to institute proceedings, but the school boards were *obliged* to do so in 'appropriate cases'. As a result of the combination of a generalised citizen right to propose a child for admission to an industrial school and a statutory responsibility for the school boards to do so the Act was, it was claimed, 'worked to the uttermost'.[4]

However, the elementary education legislation impinged upon the fortunes of the industrial schools in another important way as a result of the introduction of compulsory attendance. This brought into the industrial schools an entirely new class of children who were committed because they had failed to comply with a previously imposed attendance order. As the inspector of reformatory and industrial schools pointed out in his report for 1884: 'some of the so-called industrial schools are full of educational cases.'[5] As a means of counteracting the substantial opposition that this measure aroused, the government had hastily introduced an amendment to the 1876 Education Bill which created a new category of day industrial schools, or 'truant schools', as they came to

be known. However, they remained few in number and diverted no more
than a trickle of children from the residential industrial schools. In effect,
therefore, compulsory education and the truants whom by definition it
created, served to swell the demand for industrial school places. This
was particularly so in areas where either the school board or individual
school attendance officers (the forerunners of today's education social
workers) were vigorous in the enforcement of the rules of attendance.

Thus, the growth in the number of children in the industrial schools
until the 20th century was, in the language of today's economists, in part
demand led – but it was also led by supply. There was a notable
enthusiasm on the part of voluntary groups up and down the country
for establishing institutions. Between the years 1861 and 1884, for
example, the number of certified industrial schools in Great Britain rose
from 34 to 141.

Reasons determining length of stay in industrial schools
Just as important on the supply side of the equation for growth, however,
were the long periods that children spent in industrial schools. Many of
the children who were committed to these institutions were young. In
1880, for instance, nearly a fifth of them were under 10 years old and
roughly two-thirds were not yet 12. Even by 1913 just over half of all
the children were under 12 at admission.[6] Since children could be
detained until they were 16 their number grew by accumulation. Although
there was provision for releasing them earlier on licence (and constant
exhortation from the Home Office for institutions to do so), there were
several strong reasons for the managers to retain the children as long
as possible. The first was that, because many of the voluntary schools[7]
were in serious financial difficulty most of the time, the *per capita* grants
from the Treasury (which on average covered half of their costs) were
of the utmost importance and this income was maximised by keeping
the institutions full.

The second reason why children were retained for long periods (some
for up to 10 years) was that schools relied upon the profits from the goods
produced by the children as part of their 'industrial training'. In 1884,
for example, these represented about 7 per cent of the total income of
all the industrial schools and much more than that in some of them.[8]
However, the most productive children were, of course, the older ones.
Those of 7 or 8 could hardly have been expected to do the amount or
kind of work that could be undertaken by a 14- or 15-year-old. There
was, therefore, a special financial incentive to retain the older children

as well as to keep children who had been admitted at a young age until they were old enough to make a more valuable contribution.

It should not be assumed, of course, that the so-called industrial training introduced all children to a skilled trade. The need for industrial schools to secure contracts which brought in income, led the Royal Commission of 1884 that looked into the problems of reformatory and industrial schools to draw particular attention to the inappropriateness of some of the work that children were obliged to do:

> 'We do not regard wood-chopping and matchbox-making, which are frequently prominent amongst the trades taught, as satisfactory modes of employing the time normally devoted to industrial training . . . Still more objectionable is the occasional resort to oakum-picking or hair-teasing.'

It was also noted that, in order to raise as much income as possible, not only were children made to do inappropriate work but also to spend long periods at work to the detriment of their health and education.[9] As the first report of the new Home Office Children's Branch commented with approval in 1923:

> 'No longer is the work of the schoolroom relegated to the evenings when the child is too tired to benefit by . . . instruction.'[10]

However, the recorded profits of the children's labour underestimated its importance to the internal economies of the schools. Most labour was contributed to the running of the schools: shoemaking and repairing, tailoring, washing, ironing, knitting, darning, cleaning, and gardening were all done as part of the industrial training – but nevertheless provided valuable services for the institutions. There were also inter-institutional exchanges of labour. Girls' industrial schools took in the washing and darning from neighbouring boys' industrial schools whilst the boys could mend the girls' shoes. This was all possible because the schools were exempt from the growing body of legislation that regulated the labour of children and which imposed minimum periods of compulsory education. Of course, the rationale was that industrial training *was* a form of education – and for these children a particularly good form of education – since it prepared them for useful employment and inculcated the habit of regular work. Nevertheless it was certainly ironic that a proportion of the children who spent long hours at work away from the classroom in the industrial schools had originally been committed because they were not attending school regularly, sometimes because they were working in order to augment the family income. As a circular from the Chief Inspector insisted as late as 1919:

> 'many of the forms of occupation which have hitherto been classified as "industrial training" must be abolished or curtailed, so that time may be given to training of a higher order.'[11]

As well as the usefulness of their labour there was a third reason why the industrial schools held on to their charges when many of them might have been released earlier. Both managers and staff were often convinced that children needed to be kept apart from the damaging and corrupting influences of their parents and past associates for as long as possible. The industrial schools, as well as the reformatories, were frequently founded and run by people who were motivated by strong religious convictions and missionary zeal. Indeed, most schools remained denominational in character until the modern period. They wanted to save children both practically and spiritually. The rationale of the institution was that it enabled children's lives to be regulated, and instruction and education given undisturbed by the temptations and contaminations of the worlds from which the children had come. This had to be done, it was believed, in the controlled space of an institution. However, success could only be ensured if children were retained long enough to see them through the ages of greatest danger, that is, until they could establish a life independent of their parents. In the case of girls that almost always meant being old enough to go into residential domestic service and for many of the boys being old enough to enter the Army, the Royal Navy or the merchant navy. In short, the industrial schools wanted to keep the children until they could be settled in some work that, ideally, provided them with a livelihood and accommodation as well as a continuing source of discipline. Only in this way, it was frequently argued, could the hard-won achievements of the schools be safeguarded.

The regimes operating within industrial schools
The form which the industrial schools took has already been considered in relation to the dominance of voluntary management. There is, however, also the question of the regimes that operated within the schools. Of course it is dangerous to generalise, for many differences in detail were to be found. Nonetheless, the experience of organised work combined with conventional education were central features of the whole system.

Broadly speaking, about half of the children's time (varying with age) was supposed to be spent in industrial training and the other half in schoolroom instruction. As Rose points out, this reflected the reformers' belief in 'education and industry as a means of reclaiming the lower classes'.[12] That conviction was not unique to the industrial schools. As far as children were concerned, it found clear expression both within the Poor Law and in the manner in which care was organised by the voluntary children's societies independently of the reformatory and industrial schools. The Poor Law, for instance, made provision for the education of the children in its care well before it was made compulsory for all children. The idea that lay behind these moves was firmly embedded in the belief that, through education, the worrying cycle of pauperism could be broken, thus in the longer term removing both a public expense and a public threat. Most of the voluntary societies subscribed to the same view, with the notable addition that it was considered that through education firm and life-long religious beliefs could be instilled.

Yet, alongside this widespread confidence in the beneficial effects of education (albeit education of a rudimentary kind) there existed an even stronger belief in the necessity for the lower classes to acquire the habits of industry and to accept the discipline of wage labour. Indeed, as can be seen from the history of the Poor Law 'the principle of putting the poor of all ages to work was well accepted'.[13] In the workhouse schools, as much as in the reformatory and industrial schools, the older children spent a substantial part of their time in 'industrial training', and this was certainly a pattern that was accepted by Barnardo and similar figures in the sphere of voluntary child care. Barnardo introduced the 'half-time' system into his Homes from the outset, explaining that, whilst he valued the result of school work, he valued even more the training imparted in the trades shops.[14]

Thus, the practical value of industrial training for the children of the poor was widely applauded. But that value was enhanced, so it was believed, by the intrinsic virtue and reforming nature of work. That should surprise no-one acquainted with the pervasiveness of the work ethic in Victorian Britain. What is surprising perhaps was the widespread application of that principle to the children (and in some instances to quite young children) looked after in residential Homes of various kinds when, for other children generally, steps were being taken to limit their work in preference to their education. The reason was doubtless the strong belief in the morally regenerating influence of work for the particular group being cared for in Homes. This belief was aptly expressed by an early commentator on the industrial schools in this way:

Exercised in no useful pursuit, they must be taught to use their
hands in a number of humble but necessary duties; and as labour
is in itself virtue . . . the more they are so trained within reasonable
bounds, the better they will be prepared, under the Divine blessing,
for giving efficacy to religious instruction.[18]

II Decline and reform – the years between the Wars

Inasmuch as the reformatory and industrial schools were the products
of the particular circumstances of the middle decades of the 19th century
and subsequently changed remarkably little despite changing conditions,
their scale and importance was bound to be eroded. The Royal
Commission of 1884 was the first clear sign that all was not well and
the fact that it was followed by departmental committees of inquiry in
1895[16] and again in 1913[17] provided further evidence of continuing
disquiet. Partly because of the strong vested interests in the existing
system that were associated with the involvement of powerful figures
in its voluntary management (Lord Aberdare, for instance, was both
chairman of the 1884 Commission and of the Feltham Reformatory),
little of this disquiet led to reform. The Home Office was certainly uneasy
about the growth of the industrial schools, not least because of the
mounting cost to the public purse. The problem, however, was that the
demand for places was largely out of its control – but no alternative offered
itself. The Home Office paid the piper but was unable to call the tune.
   Nonetheless, by the 20th century a variety of social and economic
forces had begun to undermine the foundations of the system, albeit that
the 1914-18 War delayed their effect. At the turn of the century some
25,000 children were detained in reformatory or industrial schools in
England and Wales, yet, by 1930 this figure had fallen to about 6,000.
The greater part of this reduction occurred in the 1920s and was most
pronounced in the industrial schools (where the number of children fell
from 13,200 in 1918 to 3,900 in 1930), and in particular for girls in both
the reformatory and industrial schools (whose number sank from 3,000
to 900 during the same period).[18] How are these quite dramatic changes
to be explained.

Changes in the funding of industrial schools and reformatories
We have seen how the growth and maintenance of the industrial schools
had been facilitated by the availability of *per capita* grants from the Home
Office. However, there had been a longstanding wish on the part of central

government to alter this arrangement so that greater control could be exercised over both the scale of this expenditure and over the conduct of individual schools. The growing number of vacancies that many schools were experiencing, together with the diminution of voluntary donations was causing them severe financial problems. Thus, the balance of power between them and the Home Office shifted in favour of the Home Office which, immediately after the war, had the opportunity to change the method by which it gave financial support. The new scheme, introduced in 1919, divided the cost of maintaining the schools between central and local government. Henceforth, the Home Office each year set a fixed budget for every school. It also determined an average flat rate contribution that the local authorities from whose areas children were admitted had to pay. The annual amount by which this income fell short of the approved budget in any school was met by the Home Office – in effect a deficit subsidy.

This new arrangement had three consequences, First, as intended, it enabled the Home Office to exercise more control, both financially and in terms of the regulation of the schools. Secondly, it removed the incentive for the schools to take and keep as many children as possible since, at least from year to year, their approved budgets were guaranteed. Thirdly, however, because it placed a clearer, and in most cases a larger financial responsibility on the local authorities, many became less willing to bring children before the courts with a view to their being committed to an industrial school. As in so many other spheres of social policy, the manner in which systems are financed played a crucial part in determining the development of the schools. However, other forces too were leading to a reduction in the number of children being accommodated. Some of these influences dated back to before the 1914-18 War and, although their impact was not immediate, their eventual effect was considerable.

The effects of legislative reforms

One of these important factors was the increased range of options available to magistrates as a result of the implementation of the Probation of Offenders Act, 1907 and the Children Act of the following year. Lesser offences or less serious problems of behaviour could now be dealt with in ways that did not involve removing the children from home. For instance, in 1908 some 2,800 children under 16 were placed on probation; by 1926 the number had risen to 6,500; and by 1935 to 12,500.[19]

A few years later the Mental Deficiency Act of 1913 enabled mentally handicapped children to be placed in special facilities. They were gradually removed, therefore, from the industrial schools. The long-term and cumulative effect of this measure was greater than it would at first appear, since the mentally handicapped had always figured prominently amongst the long-stay children in the schools.

The Children Act of 1908 also established for the first time separate juvenile courts. Their special character took time to evolve but in London, for example, through the Juvenile Courts (Metropolis) Act of 1920, it became a requirement that juvenile courts should be presided over by a magistrate with special experience or qualifications for dealing with children and be assisted by two other justices, one of whom had to be a woman. Other cities and towns followed suit. The juvenile courts were also increasingly assisted by specially prepared reports on the child's social circumstances, health and education. A more humanitarian, informed and child-centred court system thus gradually emerged. As a result magistrates were less ready than before to make orders for the removal of children to institutions, especially for long periods and particularly young children. For example, whereas at the start of the 1920s about 20 per cent of the children in the industrial schools were under 10 this proportion had fallen to 2 per cent by 1936.[20]

The influence of changing social attitudes

Much of the legislative reform reflected more general changes in ideas about how children should be treated. Undoubtedly, more sensitive and humane attitudes developed, partly as a result of declining rates of infant and child mortality. Another factor was the expansion of teacher training that followed in the wake of the establishment of compulsory education, for this created a teaching profession that encouraged the study of children. Children began to be seen to have needs that were different from those of adults. That process was certainly retarded by the lack of opportunity for women to participate in those public affairs that concerned children. It is noteworthy that the reformatory and industrial schools remained almost wholly separate for boys and girls and that, except in the girls' schools, male staff predominated, especially in senior and management positions. Indeed, the architecture and regimes of the schools were frequently modelled on images of the boys' public school.

In addition to these changes a growing public awareness of some of the harsh and intensive treatment that was meted out in reformatory and industrial schools was reflected in a growing reluctance on the part of magistrates to commit children to such establishments. There were a number of well-publicised scandals, the most important of which was probably the case of the Akbar Nautical Training School. In 1910 the popular magazine *John Bull* charged that boys there were ill-treated to the point of torture and that some had died as a result. A committee of inquiry was established but though finding evidence of unduly severe punishment the report rejected the charges of brutality.[21] Its conclusions neither satisfied the critics nor disposed of the issue. Partly as a result, yet another departmental committee of inquiry was set up to look into all aspects of the provision and running of reformatory and industrial schools.[22] It reported in 1913 and as a result of its recommendations more stringent regulations were issued (especially about discipline and punishment). These strengthened the hand of the inspectorate which became part of the new Children's Branch of the Home Office that had been created almost immediately after the report was published.

Carlebach has argued that the Akbar affair heralded a period of growing hostility to the schools – a hostility that was expressed not only by penal reformers but by a wider public up and down the country.[23] Certainly attempts were made to improve the image of the schools, not least by their no longer being referred to as reformatory or industrial schools but rather as Home Office schools. Their association with juvenile criminality and custodial detention was played down in preference to the idea that they were providing for the child 'a good education and training in a boarding school run on public school lines'.[24]

Thus, although the disruptions of the years of the first world war deferred the impact of these various changes their effect became more clearly evident in the post-war period, coinciding with a marked fall in the number of juvenile delinquents. For example, whereas 50,000 children were proceeded against in the juvenile courts in 1918, this number had halved by 1927.[25] Of course, it was likely that this reduction was itself a reflection of changing attitudes towards juvenile offending, with the result that it was not considered necessary to bring so many children before the courts, especially for trivial offences. Furthermore, at least in the view of the Home Office, children were now 'less neglected . . . than before the war', there was 'not the same degree of poverty which then accompanied unemployment' and, because the elementary schools were more attractive, truancy had become 'almost negligible'.[26] Nonetheless, even in 1923 a quarter of all children committed to industrial schools had been sent because of their failure to attend school.[27]

Metamorphosis – approved schools
As we have seen, a combination of factors led to a substantial reduction in the number of children being sent to reformatory and industrial schools in the 1920s, especially the latter. Forty schools were closed between 1920 and 1923, leaving a total of 130 by comparison with 173 in 1915.

Several closures each year continued throughout the 1920s. There was, therefore, by the 1930s, every sign of a system in terminal decline. Its future was one aspect of the terms of reference of the Departmental Committee on the Treatment of Young Offenders that reported in 1927.[28] Three of its recommendations, eventually incorporated in the 1933 Children and Young Persons Act, did much to forestall that decline and offered the system a new lease of life. The distinction between reformatory and industrial schools disappeared and they became known as 'approved schools' and were classified according to the ages of the children they admitted. The age below which children could be committed to the schools was raised from 16 to 17, reflecting a parallel move that enabled the juvenile courts to deal with youngsters up to that age. Finally, the maximum duration of an approved school order was fixed at three years, with the expectation that the child would be released earlier on licence – a change that tended to make magistrates more favourably disposed towards the use of approved school orders.

III Another cycle – expansion and contraction

The changing character of the approved school population
The demand for approved school places mounted sharply as a result of the changes that were introduced by the Children and Young Persons Act of 1933. However, the pattern of that demand altered. For example, although by 1939 boys still outnumbered girls, the ratio fell from seven to one in 1933 to five to one in 1939. The number of girls in approved schools had nearly doubled whereas the number of boys had risen by only a third. The overall growth continued throughout the war years but the rate of increase was still more pronounced for girls than for boys – about 40 per cent to 20 per cent. By 1945, girls comprised nearly a quarter of the schools' population. As the Home Office explained:

> 'As the possibilities of action under the care or protection provisions of the Children and Young Persons Act came to be realised by local authorities and courts, immoral girls aged 16 were brought before the juvenile courts in increasing numbers. Furthermore, war-time influences, including the presence of foreign troops in this country, led to a still greater increase in the number of girls of 15 and 16 falling into immoral ways.' As a result, 'a further rapid increase in the number of senior girls' schools became necessary.'[29]

Of course, as a result of the older ages at which children could be sent to approved schools, the number of 16-year-olds coming into the schools increased. However, because children could now only be sent for a maximum period of three years, younger children did not remain long enough to become older residents. Consequently, the age structure of the schools changed only moderately. For example, in 1934 the proportion over 15 was 42 per cent, in 1938, 50 per cent and 46 per cent in 1948.[30]

The interest in such statistics lies in the extent to which they reflect changing attitudes towards both bringing children before the courts and, on the part of magistrates, to their committal to approved schools. Both sets of attitudes seem to have become more favourable after the reforms of 1933. Two factors may help to explain the change. First, more of the children placed on approved school orders were offenders. In that sense the police rather than the local authorities played the more prominent part and, unlike the local authorities (who mainly brought care or protection cases), they bore none of the financial consequences of the disposals that followed. Secondly, of course, the very fact of 16 year olds having been brought into the juvenile court system considerably increased the number of offenders that it dealt with. By 1936, 78 per cent of the children committed to approved school were offenders; in 1924, by contrast, it had been 60 per cent.[31]

The mounting number of offenders in approved schools was also influenced by the greater use made by magistrates of fit person orders that committed children in need of care or protection to local authorities. This had been encouraged by the changes of 1933. Whereas in 1936 just 822 children were subjected to such orders, by 1950 the figure had risen to 3,200.[32] These were children who, in the past, could well have been sent to industrial schools. However, more than anything else, increasing use of approved schools for offenders was influenced by a fresh surge of juvenile delinquency. The number of youngsters under 17 found guilty of indictable offences rose, for example, by three-quarters between 1938 and 1945 and high rates persisted, despite annual fluctuations, until 1951, after which they began to fall.

Because of the changing character of the intake to approved schools their futures, like those of the reformatories, became increasingly tied to the number of children brought before the courts as offenders. Thus, almost 50 new schools were provided between 1933 and 1950 as these numbers grew, whereas from 1951 to 1954, 28 were closed as they once more declined. However, juvenile delinquency almost immediately began to increase again after this, exceeding the high level of 1951 by some

5,000 in 1960. In consequence, more children were committed to approved schools and the system once more came under considerable pressure. It had 'at one and the same time to provide new accommodation, recruit extra staff [and] absorb the flood of new entrants'.[33] The response, yet again, was to embark upon new construction, conversion and enlargement. A programme was begun in 1960 that aimed to provide 20 extra schools by 1966, giving a 25 per cent increase in the places available.[34]

The effects of the new ideology on approved schools
The number of children in approved schools remained at about 7,000 to 8,000 until, in 1971, after the changes brought about by the 1969 Children and Young Persons Act and the Local Authority Social Services Act, 1970, the approved school population was merged with the general population of children in local authority care. Then, in 1974, the schools were renamed community homes with education and (although some continued to be run by voluntary societies) became absorbed into the pool of residential child care provision available to the new local authority social services departments.

These changes were not made simply for administrative convenience. Just as the fortunes of the approved schools had been affected by changing levels of juvenile delinquency, so now in the 1960s, they were to be determined by a tide of new ideas about the nature of that delinquency and what should be done about it. A renewed emphasis was placed upon the family as the location of the causes of delinquency – causes such as deprivation, disruption and neglect. Unlike the 19th century it was not concluded that the child, therefore, needed to be removed from these adverse influences but that the problem had to be tackled in the family with the help of services designed for that purpose.

In this view the young offender was the victim of circumstances that might have led to any of a number of problems. Delinquency was just one of them. It followed, therefore, that the distinction between the child in need of care or protection and the juvenile offender was artificial, misleading and unhelpful. The steps that needed to be taken to prevent child deprivation and neglect would serve equally well to forestall delinquency, for they shared a common root.[35]

These convictions were closely related to the desire to protect the child, and especially the young child, from the stigma of criminality and, therefore, from the necessity for him to be exposed to the formality of a court appearance. There was pressure to raise the age of criminal responsibility from 8 to at least 12, as well as encouragement for a greater use of cautioning by the police and other forms of community-based 'deflection' – such as intermediate treatment. Clearly, in this approach to juvenile offending, there was to be a much reduced role for all forms of detention.

Of course, these views were not shared by everyone. However, they came to exercise political influence because they were incorporated as part of the Labour Party's policies for dealing with crime – policies which, though thrashed out in opposition, accompanied the party to power in 1964.[36] Exactly how these ideas found their way into the party's policies is a fascinating story that cannot be told here. Suffice it to say that contemporary sociological and criminological theories, especially those concerned with 'labelling' and the social construction of deviance, played their part – as did a concern with the disproportionate number of children in all forms of detention who came from poor and disadvantaged backgrounds. At the next stage, however, it was of crucial importance that those who had been involved in the search for new policies whilst in opposition went on to occupy key positions in the new government and were able, therefore, to sustain the impetus for reform.

Even so, that impetus was retarded by powerful interests that considered that the proposed reforms went too far, too quickly. Compromises had to be made as evidenced by the publication of a second, and much revised, white paper on the subject.[37] Nevertheless, many of the original proposals survived in the 1969 Children and Young Persons Act although with its implementation passing into the hands of a Conservative government that was far from committed to its principles, important sections of the legislation were never put into practice. Nevertheless, enough was done to bring to an end the approved school system as it had been known. Approved school orders were replaced by much more general care orders which simply committed children to a local authority's care without specifying where or how they should be accommodated. The schools became part of the stock of community Homes (although in most cases continuing to provide education on the premises). The Home Office no longer carried an overall responsibility for the establishments although, for a number of years, their utilisation was guided by regional planning committees.

Other factors involved in the demise of approved schools

Both before and during these changes, the position of the approved schools had been weakened by factors other than the new ideology. First, since the 1950s their rates of 'success' as measured by the level of reoffending amongst youngsters who had been discharged began to fall – eventually quite significantly. Whereas in the past they had been able to defend their contribution by reference to low rates of reoffending, this indicator now became a liability. Secondly, their costs had risen. Thirdly, they had been undermined by a series of scandals that culminated in the inquiry in 1967 into excessive punishment at the Court Lees Approved School.[38]

For some years after the radical reforms of the early 1970s the newly-entitled community homes with education continued to play an important part in total child care provision. The pressure on places was considerable as the numbers in care rose to a peak in 1978 before what was to become a dramatic reduction began in the 1980s. This, together with their continually escalating cost, the increasing sale value of the sites they occupied, the declining number of offenders being committed to care, the increasing emphasis on boarding-out as well as upon returning children home as soon as possible, led many local authorities and voluntary societies to close their CHEs. Demand had slumped. Whereas at the turn of the century there had been some 25,000 youngsters in reformatory and industrial schools in England and Wales, and 9,000 in 1952 in their successors the approved schools, by 1977 the number in CHEs had fallen to 6,500 and by 1986 to fewer than 2,000.

The origins of the reformatory and industrial schools lay in a particular period of the 19th century. Partly because of its geographically scattered and enclosed character, and partly because of the structure of interests that surrounded it, the system was essentially conservative and slow to change. When change did occur it was often by way of a reluctant response to external pressures. Although some schools made important and progressive alterations in their regimes, the system as a whole came to be driven first by one wind and then by another. When opportunities for change and redirection occurred they were rarely taken. Throughout their existence, the purpose of the schools remained the control of juveniles, both for the protection of society (as it was seen) and in order to achieve lasting changes in the children's behaviour. The latter aim came to be expounded as the principal rationale so that once their effectiveness in doing this came to be doubted, and the rightness of residential separation seriously challenged, the schools became deeply vulnerable to the cost calculators.

Whatever their shortcomings, however, the schools did protect thousands of children from the horrors of the penal system, they kept them out of trouble for a few years and, until the collapse of manufacturing industry, they equipped many of them to obtain jobs when they left. More than a few came to be run with great enthusiasm, optimism, sensitivity and pride, although by the 1960s it was clear that morale was fast declining in the face of an uncertain and threatened future.

4 The boarding-out of poor law children – a mirror on residential care

I Poor law children in the 19th century

The promotion of boarding-out

Little attention was paid to boarding-out as a method of providing for poor law children in England and Wales until the 1860s, when the number of children under the age of 16 in poor law institutions rose steadily from some 43,000 at the beginning of the decade until, by 1869, it had reached an unprecedented peak of 58,000. The extra numbers, together with the growing insistence that children should be kept separate from adult paupers, confronted many boards of guardians with the prospect of having to embark upon new building programmes. Boarding-out began to find favour as a less expensive solution to the problem. Had the numbers continued their upward course, the financial argument might well have accelerated this development. As it was the economy began to pick up after 1870, the number of children in the care of the guardians fell and the pressure on accommodation eased.

Nevertheless, the campaign for boarding-out that had been mounted by a group of influential ladies in the latter years of the 1860s (and which was to become the National Committee for Promoting the Boarding-out of Pauper Children) was sustained. Florence Davenport Hill's book, *Children of the State* (published in 1868),[1] provided much of the evidence upon which those who advocated boarding-out relied. A major theme was the need to protect young children – and especially girls – from the damaging effects of institutional life. Indeed, the boarding-out associations which were formed by groups of middle-class women in various areas were frequently the result of their disquiet at what they saw as members of local workhouse visiting societies.

Yet, as a class, these ladies were also keenly aware of the shortage of reliable domestic servants. Boarding-out offered a promising means whereby pauper girls might be rescued from the adverse influences of workhouse surroundings and, at the same time, be fitted for employment by the lower ranks of the servant-keeping classes. It was believed that an infusion of additional labour at this level would have a generally beneficial effect by increasing the overall supply.

However, it must be borne in mind that the campaign was chiefly aimed at persuading the central Poor Law Board (and later, its successor, the Local Government Board) to permit unions to board-out children beyond their boundaries. Guardians could already place children in foster homes within their area without such permission. The idea was that children should be removed from the physically and morally dangerous surroundings of the cities to the countryside, where they could live with respectable cottagers.

Hence, there were several interwoven threads in the case that was made for boarding-out. Different emphases were used in different settings and, of course, different aspects appealed to different groups. Whatever the arguments used by a deputation of lady lobbyists to the president of the Poor Law Board in 1870, they met with some success.[2] The group delivered a petition signed by over 3,000 other ladies. It was agreed that the Board would allow a limited experiment in boarding-out 'beyond the union', and a General Order to that effect was issued in the same year.

The distrust of boarding-out expressed by the Poor Law Board

The concession was made with a good deal of reluctance for although it was acknowledged that a properly conducted system of boarding-out could bestow great benefits on pauper children, it was also considered to be open to 'abuses of a deplorable character' and 'result in moral and social evils of the greatest magnitude'.[3] These fears were expressed by the Board's secretariat and especially by its inspectors. Their misgivings were of two kinds. First, there were those that sprang from a pervading concern with efficiency, which was seen to be secured mainly by successfully controlling the use of poor relief. That, in its turn, meant avoiding any major departures from the principle of less eligibility as well as retaining as much central control over local activities as possible. Boarding-out was regarded as a dangerous deviation from these objectives. In particular, the condition of the boarded-out child might be seen to be more favourable than that of the child of the poor but 'independent' labourer. The alarming conclusion drawn by the Board's officers was that more parents would be encouraged to seek poor relief by the prospect of their child being boarded-out in a comfortable cottage home.

Yet it would be a mistake to believe that the central Board, at least in the persons of its senior civil servants and inspectors, took this negative view of boarding-out only because they feared that it would threaten the principle of less eligibility. They also expressed anxieties that in placing children outside the unions – often at considerable distances – the guardians would not be able to exercise adequate supervision over their treatment and general well-being. In the workhouse or district schools, attendance was assured, over-work could be proscribed and proper food and clothing made subject to detailed regulation. Boarding-out carried with it unknown risks and dangers which would not be easy to detect or to correct. Worst of all the inspectors could not oversee what went on in the same way that they could when children were collected together in institutions.

Some regulations and restraints applied to boarding-out

The general distrust of boarding-out that was felt by the central Board's officers was vividly reflected in the limited coverage of the 1870 Order and in the detailed regulations that it contained. Boarding-out beyond the union was only to be allowed in a limited number of unions, mostly in the congested urban areas. These authorities were permitted to place children outside their areas provided that they had made arrangements with a voluntary boarding-out committee in the reception area which was prepared to find foster homes and offer supervision. The children were to be visited at least at six-weekly intervals. In order to prevent any possibility of 'farming-out', not more than two children were to be placed in any one home unless they were brothers and sisters. All boarding-out in larger towns (of over 15,000) was to be avoided. School attendance was to be compulsory (remember that it was not yet compulsory for other children) and placements were not to be more than a mile and a half from a school. The schoolmaster was to furnish quarterly reports on the child's progress and proper provision had to be made for the child's medical treatment.

Not all children were to be eligible for boarding-out – only those who were 'practically orphans' (because of a parent's death, desertion or permanent disability). This was 'to avoid severing or weakening in any way the ties of family, even where, owing to the character of the parents, it might be thought that children would be benefited by removal from their control'.[4] Guardians were to board-out the eligible children as early as possible after 2 years of age, but not later than 10. In order that the committees could keep an adequate oversight of children in remote areas, no child was to be placed in a home which was further than five miles away from that of some member of the committee.[5] The foster parents were also required to sign a detailed undertaking which specified their responsibilities and which set out the terms upon which they received the child (a maximum payment of four shillings a week was to be allowed, plus clothing allowances, medical and school fees).

These remarkably detailed regulations covered all the possibilities of neglect or ill-usage that administrators at the commencement of the 1870s could have been expected to foresee. They imposed a standard which, if achieved in practice, certainly placed the well-being of the boarded-out child at a level well beyond what might have been supposed to have breached the principle of less eligibility. Thus the regulations are a good illustration of the tension that existed in the central poor law administration throughout the last quarter of the 19th century; a tension between the legacy of 1834 (with all its trappings of less eligibility, means-testing and fear of abuse of the system) and the concern to safeguard the well-being of children who were the responsibility of a multitude of individual boards of guardians which were often regarded as potentially wayward and slack in their administration.

Failures alleged in the boarding-out systems
The scepticism and suspicion with which the poor law inspectorate continued to regard boarding-out throughout the 1870s and '80s are exemplified in many of their papers. For example, Andrew Doyle, the Inspector for Wales, prepared a report in 1875 on how the system was operating in Swansea.[6] The Swansea guardians had rejected his proposal to join with other unions to build a district school on the cottage home pattern. They argued that they were pursuing the alternative policy of boarding-out. Doyle, however, contended that they had only done so in order to avoid upgrading their workhouse and having to make separate residential provision for children. He visited all the children boarded-out (most of whom were in the town) and compiled a catalogue of unsatisfactory conditions. These included the exploitation of children's labour by foster parents; gross over-crowding; irregular school attendance; and poverty-stricken surroundings.

Partly as a result of Doyle's report the Local Government Board took new steps in 1877 to control boarding-out within the unions. A similar Order was issued to the one that had been drawn up in 1870 to control boarding-out beyond the union. However, there were certain differences. No age restrictions were imposed and instead of a boarding-out committee undertaking the supervision, it was to be done by a relieving officer and the medical officer of health.

These regulations were introduced in order to combat what the central Board saw as great laxity in the way that local boards of guardians exercised their responsibility for ensuring the well-being of boarded-out children in their care. They were not intended to promote boarding-out within the unions. Indeed, there was such general concern about the low standards of care offered in foster homes that a special woman inspector was appointed in 1885 with an exclusive responsibility for visiting those children boarded-out beyond the union boundaries. For example, the central Board concluded from her second annual report that a 'strong warning is necessary for the protection of children against ill-treatment or neglect by persons who have taken them for use or profit'.[7]

The unexpected expansion of the boarding-out system

With notable exceptions, like Liverpool and Birmingham, there was as little enthusiasm for boarding-out beyond their unions amongst boards of guardians as there was at the Local Government Board. Even by 1880, only 500 children were placed at long distance and although the figure doubled in the next five years it never matched the scale of boarding-out within unions. For example, in 1877 of the 93 boarding-out committees that had been approved by the Local Government Board only 49 were actually responsible for any children. Ladies in the country towns and rural areas were more ready to form committees than the urban guardians were to use them.

However, in spite of the misgivings about boarding-out expressed by the central department and its inspectorate and the reluctance of many local guardians to do other than use the places in institutions that were available to them, boarding-out began to emerge as a distinctive system for looking after poor law children from about the middle years of the 1880s. In 1887 there were 3,300 poor law children in foster homes in England and Wales, or 11 per cent of the total. By the outbreak of war in 1914, there were 11,600 or 26 per cent of all those for whom the guardians were responsible. There were several reasons for this development.

By the first years of the 1880s, following rapidly rising unemployment in 1878 and 1879, the number of children in the care of the Poor Law began to mount once again, rising to a new peak in 1888. Thereafter, except for a few years, the upward trend continued until, in 1913, boards of guardians were responsible for 84,000 children. The conflict between providing sufficient places in institutions and developing boarding-out was resolved – boarding-out was seen as preferable to the new capital investment that would have been required to accommodate the rising tide of children. However, there were also other forces at work.

Compulsory education
Although full-time education up to the age of 14 did not become universal in England and Wales until 1918, an Act to make it compulsory between

the ages of 5 and 10 was passed in 1880. The chances that the boarded-out child would be sent to school were thereby increased. The claim that only by being in a poor law residential school could the education of the poor law child be ensured, began to lose its force. This was important since, as we have seen, education was regarded by the central Poor Law authority as the most effective means of breaking the cycle of pauperism.

Partly for these reasons the scope of boarding-out was extended by new regulations issued in 1889. Additional classes of children became eligible to be boarded-out, most notably those who would henceforth be 'adopted' by guardians as a result of the 1889 Poor Law (Amendment) Act which, for the first time, allowed boards to assume parental rights and duties over children who were orphans or whose parents were unable or unfit to look after them.

Changes in attitudes within the local boards of guardians
The critics of institutional care sitting on local boards of guardians also became more numerous, especially as more women were elected. The cause of boarding-out, particularly for girls, was now more often championed by women from within the poor law system rather than by those at a distance who lacked any political foothold in the local administration.

The Mundella Report, 1896
The boarding-out system received additional encouragement from the publication in 1896 of the Mundella Report on the maintenance and education of poor law children in the metropolis.[8] The commissioners recommended that boarding-out should be expanded and suggested, amongst other things, that more women inspectors should be appointed (a proposal that was duly accepted); that the age restrictions should be removed (something that was not done until 1911); and that the limit of four shillings a week, which the guardians were allowed to pay foster parents, should be removed in the case of children under 2 or for those who had special needs (another proposal that was not taken up).

The rise and subsequent fall in the number being boarded-out
Yet despite these favourable influences the women inspectors of boarding-out continued to emphasise its disadvantages and risks as much as its advantages. They were particularly concerned with the motives of foster parents. Notwithstanding such misgivings over a quarter of poor law children were boarded-out by the outbreak of war in 1914 and the central authority had cleared away many of the restrictions that had formerly

been imposed. However, they still insisted that only orphans, deserted, or illegitimate children and those for whom the guardians had assumed parental rights could be placed with foster parents. Even so, there seemed no reason why, after the disruptions caused by the war, the use of foster care should not continue to grow. That did not happen. Indeed, the number of children boarded-out dropped from 12,000 in 1914 to about 9,000 in 1920, rose slightly to 10,500 in 1925 but then fell again to 6,000 by 1939 – a level similar to that which had prevailed in the middle years of the 1890s. Why was this?

II Poor law children – the inter-war years

The decline in the boarding-out of poor law children
One obvious reason for the decline in the number of poor law children boarded-out between the wars was that the number of children in care declined. By 1920 it had fallen dramatically by over 20,000 since the pre-war years. Further reductions occurred, particularly after 1927, so that by 1939 there were only 37,500 children in the care of public assistance authorities in England and Wales; that is, about 45 per cent of the level in 1913. It was inevitable, therefore, that some reduction in the number of children who were boarded-out would occur – but the decline was disproportionately large. Whereas one in four of all poor law children were boarded-out in 1913 this ratio had fallen to one in six by 1939. Obviously, other factors were also at work.

It has been suggested that the local guardians only turned to boarding-out when their institutions were full.[9] Consequently, as there were fewer children to be looked after during the 1920s and 1930s so the incentive to find foster homes would have been weakened. Unlike the period after the last war residential homes were relatively cheap to run: the largely female staff were plentiful and poorly paid; the children contributed their labour to the running of the establishment; the historic debt on the buildings was comparatively low and, by the standards of the time, many of the structures were not considered to be in need of major repair. There were no pressing reasons to close homes in favour of boarding-out. The value of the land upon which they stood was very low compared with the heights reached in the 1980s and, in any case, local committees often regarded their institutions with pride and as showpieces of civic responsibility and achievement. However, by the 1930s the picture became more complicated than this analysis suggests.

The Local Government Act, 1929

The implementation in April 1930 of the Local Government Act, 1929, was an important event in the history of the public child care services. Under its provisions county councils and county borough councils took over the functions of the boards of guardians. Public assistance committees were established and in some cases they delegated several of their tasks to the councils' education or health committees.

An important result of this major reform was that the responsible authorities, especially in the conurbations and the counties, became much larger units of administration. In London, for example, the LCC assumed responsibilities that had previously been carried by 25 separate boards of guardians. This provided the opportunity for a considerable pooling of institutional resources, and therefore, with the firm encouragement of the Ministry of Health (to whom the responsibilities of the Local Government Board had passed) a more detailed classification of Homes and residential schools. It also provided the chance to close the least suitable Homes and to remove children who still remained (illegally) in the general workhouses. In the first five years after the introduction of the new arrangements 120 children's Homes were closed; some were sold and some were put to other purposes.[10]

Yet there is little evidence that this was achieved by the increased use of boarding-out. Typically, the thrust of reform was to replace the old, large-scale accommodation with smaller units. These were either private houses (collectively termed 'scattered Homes') purchased quite cheaply in a depressed housing market, or small grouped cottage Homes. The combined effect of a reduced number of children in care, a larger pool of residential accommodation, the low cost of large private houses and new building continued to make it relatively easy (despite the economic stringencies under which local authorities were obliged to work during the 1930s) to close unfit or redundant Homes without resort to boarding-out. Nevertheless, there were a few areas, notably London, where special efforts were made to increase the use of boarding-out alongside these developments.

However, at least four other factors also need to be taken into account if a convincing explanation for the failure of the public sector to develop boarding-out during the inter-war years is to be found.

Existing vacancies in voluntary Homes

One was the availability of an alternative overflow system. As we have seen, in 1931 there were some 250 voluntary Homes certified for the use of the public assistance committees. Many had vacancies. The

Ministry of Health's annual report for 1931–32 pointed out that these were Homes which authorities could use in suitable cases if they were unable to incur the expenditure necessary in making provision of their own.[11]

The absence of special staff to handle boarding-out

A second factor that contributed to the tardy development of boarding-out has been touched on already for the earlier period; namely, the absence of any special staff to engage in the recruitment of foster parents or to undertake the subsequent supervision. In 1934, for example, although 27 councils and 47 county borough councils employed women officers who devoted part of their time to boarding-out visiting, they were usually health visitors, district nurses, assistant relieving officers or clerical assistants. In the remaining 26 authorities, the visiting was done by women members of the boarding-out committees (by then sub-committees of the public assistance committees).[12]

The absence of adequate supervision of foster parents

The problem of adequate supervision was another factor that retarded the development of boarding-out. Indeed, it was this probably more than anything else that deterred the Ministry of Health from lending its support to its promotion. Instead, advice and guidance were concentrated on the reform and improvement of residential care. The attitude was almost certainly reinforced by the results of a general survey of boarding-out that inspectors had conducted in 1934. Its main conclusion was that it was important to have 'regular and systematic inspection by a visitor sufficiently trained and experienced to protect the child from a plausible foster mother who might deceive the kindly and well-meaning visitor' and that 'whilst boarding-out with a good foster mother is almost certainly the best means of dealing with the normal child who is left without parents of its own, this system can be a real danger unless properly super-vised'.[13] Echoes of the misgivings that had been expressed repeatedly by the 19th century poor law inspectors continued to be heard; indeed, after the 1934 report they became distinctly louder.

The concept of the 'unfit' child

A fourth factor that impeded the development of foster care between the wars was the prevailing notion that some children were unfit to be placed in private homes. The practical manifestation of this was to be found in the longstanding requirement that the local medical officer of health had to certify that a child was physically and mentally fit to be fostered. Obviously, different doctors interpreted this injunction differently but, to all intents and purposes, it debarred those who suffered from chronic illnesses as well as the physically and mentally handicapped. Many children who were certified as mentally defective were supported by the public assistance authorities and perhaps as many as 1,500 were accommodated in workhouses and children's homes.[14] Furthermore, it must be remembered that there was a profusion of specialised Homes in the voluntary sector to which the public assistance committees could send the deaf and dumb, the blind, the crippled or the delicate children who were in their care. There was also a general view that older youngsters were difficult to place and that 'coloured' children could hardly be placed at all.[15]

Boarding-out and war orphans

Several things suggest that the rather pessimistic view taken centrally and often locally about the feasibility of developing boarding-out was misplaced. One piece of evidence was the fact that since 1917 a parallel system of public child care had existed under the auspices of the Ministry of Pensions in order to care for war orphans. By 1920 the system was responsible for about 14,000 children. All these children were boarded-out. There were two main reasons for this. First, the Ministry of Pensions had no residential resources at its disposal and it was loath to use the poor law system for the children of those who had died for their country. Secondly, many of the children in its care were being looked after by relatives. Nevertheless, in some areas the Ministry of Pensions' regional children's officers (working to a central children's branch) competed with the poor law boarding-out committees for foster homes – indeed, it was because of this that in the early 1920s local guardians were released from the constraint of a nationally determined maximum boarding-out allowance. Of course, the number of children for whom the Ministry of Pensions was responsible gradually declined but they still had 11,000 children under their wing in 1930 and the Second World War raised the otherwise dwindling number to 7,000 by 1946.[16]

The Children and Young Persons Act, 1933, and compulsory boarding-out

After the 1933 Children and Young Persons Act the Home Office joined the Ministry of Pensions as an active supporter of boarding-out. It had been possible since 1889 for the courts to commit to the care of a 'fit person' children who had been cruelly treated and, later, those who had been neglected. Sometimes they went to the voluntary societies, sometimes to individuals and sometimes to the poor law authorities. The Home Office retained overall responsibility. The Act of 1933 did three things:

- it discouraged the committal of children to individuals
- 'it allowed courts to make certain offenders the subject of a fit person order
- it obliged local authorities (except in special circumstances and with the Home Secretary's consent) to board-out all children committed to their care under these provisions.

In fact, few children were committed on such orders initially, but the number of them in care rose rapidly because they usually stayed until they were 18.

By 1945 there were 10,000 children who had been committed to the care of the local authorities and another 3,000 for whom voluntary societies had been made responsible.[17] Of the 10,000 local authority children 60 per cent were in foster homes compared with just 15 per cent of the children who had been received under the provisions of the Poor Law. Obviously the 60 per cent rate of boarding-out fell short of what had been intended in the 1933 Act but, given that many of the children were older and that the war years had created much disruption, it was a remarkably high level. Nonetheless, the obligation to board-out all committed children was criticised by the Curtis Committee, which reported on the care of children in 1946. They felt, they said, 'obliged to deprecate insistence by the central department on the boarding-out of any particular class of children'. It was appreciated that the policy had 'led to a useful development of the boarding-out system' but it was feared that it had 'also had the effect of causing sub-standard homes to be too readily accepted'.[18]

Finally, the rather pessimistic attitude of public assistance committees to the possibility of obtaining foster homes was belied by the advancing shadow of war. By 1939 the Refugee Children's Movement had placed some 9,000 young victims of Nazi tyranny in British foster homes. In the same year, of course, the evacuation of children from the towns to the country began on an unprecedented scale. Somehow, and not always willingly, thousands upon thousands of householders in the reception areas were persuaded to accept the cohorts of children that descended upon their localities.[19] Under these circumstances it is not surprising that evacuation did little to promote the cause of foster care, either then or later. Furthermore, since many urban areas were considered to be unsafe, children in care also had to go with their Home when it was evacuated to other premises in the reception areas. The competition for places in private homes in these localities was (at least in the early years of the war) intense, and superimposed on that was the shortage of staff caused by the various aspects of mobilisation. It was for reasons like these that there was no increase during the war in the number of children in care who were placed in foster homes despite the fact that there were some 10,000 more of them being looked after by the local authorities at the end of hostilities than in 1939.

Foster care might also have been expected to have received a major set-back as a result of the much-publicised death of 13-year-old Dennis O'Neill in January 1945 from starvation and beating at the hands of his foster father. The tragedy seemed to confirm the misgivings that had been repeatedly expressed about the quality of foster homes and the standard of their supervision. Dennis and his older brother Terence had been committed to care and were therefore subject to the Home Office injunction that all such children should be boarded-out.[20]

The death of Dennis O'Neill and the widespread disenchantment amongst many of those who had had to look after evacuees hardly augured well for a vigorous post-war policy to encourage boarding-out. Indeed, during the war hundreds of hostels and nurseries had had to be established in and around the reception areas in order to cope with evacuees whose placements had failed and whose behaviour was considered to be too difficult for householders to tolerate.

However, other forces were propelling foster care into a cental position in post-war child care policy. Plans for the break-up of the Poor Law had begun to be made from 1943 onwards. If there were to be a national insurance system such as Beveridge envisaged, it would largely supplant the income maintenance work of public assistance. That meant that its other functions – the care of the old and children in particular – had to be reallocated in the administrative uncoupling of care from the payment of cash. Proposals were prepared within government for the establishment of county and county borough children's committees that would have an exclusive responsibility for separated children. However, a protracted battle developed in Whitehall about which central department would have overall responsibility. The triangular contest involved the Home Office, the Ministry of Health and (at a later stage) the Ministry of Education. In the end, and after disputation at the cabinet level, the Home Office, with its already established children's branch, emerged as the victor. This was important to the future of boarding-out since, as it will be recalled, of the two central departments then responsible for child care, the Home Office was much more enthusiastic about boarding-out than the Ministry of Health.

These developments occurred in 1947. In the meantime a powerful group of child care lobbyists, almost all of whom were women, had launched a campaign for the better care of children, especially young children. The Women's Group on Public Welfare was prominent and so too was the National Council for Maternity and Child Welfare. The child guidance movement was important as were a number of individual psychologists, magistrates and educationalists. The best known example of the considerable pressure that they were able to exert was Lady Allen of Hurtwood's letter to *The Times* in July 1944 calling for a committee of inquiry into the poor standards and lack of integration of services for deprived children. A well-orchestrated stream of letters from eminent figures followed in support. The target of the attack was principally the ill-effects of institutional life upon the mental health and sound development of young children. It was mainly as an outcome of this sustained pressure that a committee of inquiry was announced in December 1944.

The report of the Curtis Committee, 1946

The Curtis Committee delivered its report in September 1946.[21] The companion report on Scotland (Clyde) came somewhat later.[22] Apart from proposing the creation of separate children's departments in all counties and county boroughs the Curtis Report did three things that were to steer child care policy clearly towards a preference for boarding-out over all other forms of care.

First, although it was acknowledged that standards were not universally bad, the report catalogued grave deficiencies in residential care, both in the public and in the voluntary sectors. Not only were many buildings quite inadequate but the regimes were often unimaginative, harsh and stultifying. There was frequently insufficient staff and virtually none were trained. Many proposals were made for improvements.

Secondly, although foster care was regarded as the best way of providing for separated children, major criticisms were made of the way in which foster homes were selected and supervised. It was made plain, therefore, that only when children were 'suitable' and only where 'entirely satisfactory' homes could be found should boarding-out be arranged. Yet such criteria could only be met if every children's officer had available to her a staff of trained boarding-out visitors. So, thirdly, detailed proposals were made as to how such training should be organised.[23] Courses would be located in universities and recruitment was to be under the guidance of a central council and aimed at those who already had relevant background qualifications – people such as graduates in psychology or philosophy, those with social science diplomas or certificates, trained health visitors, non-graduate trained teachers and so on. Courses were to last a year. The training of well-educated people in specially designed university courses was the precondition for the 'safe' development of foster care as the flagship of child care policy. These recommendations were adopted and an emergency programme launched soon afterwards. It laid the foundation for a profession of child care that, in time, was to make a major contribution to the establishment of the wider profession of social work.

III Boarding-out and the new children's departments

With some notable exceptions, the recommendations of the Curtis Committee were incorporated in the Children Act, 1948 and in terms of the treatment of children in the care of local authorities, boarding-out was accorded pride of place. In the explanatory circular that accompanied the Act, authorities were urged 'to use every effort to arrange for boarding-out in suitable cases'.[24] This set the scene for what was to become a vigorous campaign, especially on the part of the Home Office children's department that now had overall national responsibility. As well as the factors that have already been discussed two others imparted a special impetus to this policy in the years that followed.

Post-war pressures on building
First, there were the acute shortages of building materials and building labour and the high priority that had to be given to housing repairs and then to the housing drive. For instance, after stressing the value of boarding-out for the child a Home Office circular in 1952 pointed out that the 'expansion of boarding-out should relieve pressure on accommodation in children's homes and residential nurseries, at a time when restrictions on capital investment limit severely the improvement of existing premises'.[25] These constraints lasted at least until the mid-1950s and meant that it was difficult to improve or replace existing residential accommodation; but the number of children in care rose sharply from the end of the war until 1953, thereafter remaining at much the same level until the second half of the 1960s. If the aim to avoid placing or retaining children in unsuitable or overcrowded residential accommodation

was to be realised then many of the extra children had to be found foster homes. As the Home Office pointed out in 1951, 'in most areas all the children's homes are full, and in some areas the number coming into care is rising, with the result that newly acquired premises are immediately filled up', adding that 'an important contribution to the solution of the problem of unsatisfactory buildings is to pursue a vigorous boarding-out policy.'[26]

Economic factors

The second factor that served to promote boarding-out, and one that is still influential today, was the happy coincidence (or so it seemed) that the most desirable provision was also the most economical. For example, the 1952 Home Office circular ended by emphasising that:

> 'boarding-out is the least expensive method of child care both in money and manpower, and in the present financial condition of the country it is imperative to exercise the strictest economy consistent with a proper regard for the interests of the children.'

Policy decisions on boarding-out

The policy of boarding-out also received substantial support from the Select Committee on Estimates whose report on the child care service was also published in 1952. It emphasised, for instance, that:

> 'local authorities are under a specific obligation to use boarding-out as the normal method of providing for children in their care with an implied obligation to give it an overriding priority and to make it the main objective of all their work in this connection'.[27]

In their departmental reply to this report the Home Office claimed that they were:

> 'at one with the Committee in wanting to secure a large expansion of boarding-out and to see this achieved in all suitable cases, bearing in mind that expansion cannot be forced unduly without risk of unsuitable placings and consequent damage to the children.'

And added that they would:

> 'issue renewed instructions to local authorities to the effect that boarding-out is, with due safeguards, the primary objective.'[28]

Factors affecting the expansion of foster care policies

Some local authorities, however, embraced this policy more whole-heartedly than others. Some faced different local traditions and different attitudes towards fostering, whilst some had better opportunities for recruiting foster parents than others. It did not follow that because the Home Office continually emphasised the policy, individual children's committees of the county councils and county borough councils accepted it blindly, ignoring local conditions and their own beliefs and attitudes. Rates of boarding-out varied considerably between authorities. For example, in England and Wales in 1952 the highest rate was 82 per cent and the lowest 20 per cent.[29]

Nonetheless, despite considerable encouragement and chivying from the Home Office through its inspectors, neither the number nor the rate of children boarded-out increased very much after an initial surge that seemed to have been exhausted by about 1954. For example, the rate of fostering only rose from 45 per cent in that year to a peak of 48 per cent in 1964, after which it declined steadily and continued to do so throughout the 1970s. In 1974 the rate stood at 32 per cent – roughly what it had been at the inauguration of the Children Act in 1948. Given the enthusiasm with which the policy of foster care was embraced in the post-war years, how is the failure to continue its expansion through the 1960s and 1970s to be explained? As is so often the case, there is no straightforward answer, but several intermingling factors can be identified.

The shortage of trained child care officers

The new child care training courses were seen as the means of providing the officers through whose endeavours the expansion of foster care was to be achieved. Even so, the output of the courses was not large. Up to the end of 1954, for example, 436 students (94 per cent of them women) had been trained;[30] but there were 146 children's departments in England and Wales to absorb them. Even by 1960, only 28 per cent of the child care officers working in local government were trained. Given the considerable emphasis placed upon the necessity for the expansion of foster care only to be undertaken if there were enough specially trained staff, the hesitation of some children's officers to proceed without them is understandable. At the same time the tasks of child care officers were becoming more diverse than the authors of the Curtis Report had foreseen. More work was being done with the families of children and with children who were not in care. There were also responsibilities for adoption and for working with children in residential Homes. So there was other work to be done besides finding and supervising foster homes.

The graduation of boarding-out visitors to child care officers became more than a change of title; it reflected a much wider range of responsibilities.

The scarcity of satisfactory foster parents

Satisfactory foster parents also seemed to be in short supply, particularly in some areas. The need to understand how that supply might be increased was one of the reasons that prompted the Home Office to ask the Government Social Survey to undertake a study of the recruitment of foster parents. The results were published in 1957[31] and represent the first systematic study of fostering in this country. Although the report drew no conclusions nor offered any suggestions for action, a profile of the foster mothers did emerge. Three-fifths of them were over 40 when the child in the sample was placed. Half had no other children at home and over a third were childless. One in eight had an adopted child living with them and, in all, a third had considered, or were considering, adoption. Virtually none was in paid employment. Most were working-class, although both extremes of income were under represented – the upper income groups appreciably so.

The evidence suggested two conclusions of importance. One was that the recruitment of foster mothers (little was said about foster fathers although almost all the women were married) drew upon a comparatively narrow band in terms of social class, age and family composition. The second conclusion was that foster homes were, in the terms that Holman was later to use to classify different styles of fostering, 'exclusive'.[32] They were typically long-term and adoption-like. For example, the survey found that 80 per cent of the foster children had no contact with their mothers during the time they had been in the foster homes and that mothers had only visited 4 per cent on a regular basis. Since so many of the foster homes at this time had the appearance of being pseudo-adoptions, the centrality of the policy of boarding-out almost certainly served to extend the long period of severance that we have already described.

Of course, the more fostering that was long-term, the fewer foster parents there were who could be used several times over. That increased the scarcity, as did the fact that the rule about not having more than two foster children at one time (unless they were brothers and sisters) was not lifted until the boarding-out regulations were revised in 1955.[33] However, the scarcity began to be accentuated by far-reaching economic changes that sprang from the replacement of manufacture by service industries.

The 'traditional' foster mothers who were portrayed in the Social Survey's study were members of a generation in which it was uncommon for working-class wives to go out to work. From the 1960s onwards a new generation of wives was emerging who were occupied in, or intending to return to, the paid labour market which was increasingly anxious to recruit them, albeit often on a part-time basis. Where the rates of female participation in paid work were high, or climbing, local authorities were liable to find recruitment difficult unless the boarding-out payments compared favourably with prevailing wages – and, of course, few if any of them did.

The shortage of foster parents was also aggravated by the acute post-war housing problem in many areas, particularly in those places worst affected by enemy action during the war. Slum conditions and overcrowding were often widespread in just the localities from which children were most likely to come into care. The post-war slum clearance drive did not really begin until about 1955, much of it leading to the cramped high-rise developments of the 1960s. Without some space to spare, families could not readily contemplate having a foster child and, in any case, they may not have been approved without it.

Understanding the nature of the shortage of foster homes

In endeavouring to understand the nature of the post-war shortage of foster homes (or shortage at any other time for that matter) account must also be taken of the rate at which they broke down. This affected supply in two ways. First, when foster homes collapsed, for whatever reason, they were unlikely to be used again – they disappeared from the pool. Secondly, since many children returned to residential care when breakdown occurred, there was a recirculation of demand if they were to be fostered again.

A series of studies of foster care reported their findings in the 1960s and all indicated high rates of breakdown. In 1960 Trasler estimated that between a third and two-fifths of all long-term placements were unsuccessful[34] and my work, at about the same time, found a failure rate in one county of 48 per cent.[35] At the end of the decade George reported the results of his study in three areas and these showed an overall breakdown rate of 60 per cent.[36] Whatever reservations there were about how success and failure were defined, the size of the problem of failure was obviously considerable. More caution began to be taken about pressing ahead with the 'league table' of boarding-out, in which high rates were considered to indicate that a children's department was both progressive and successful.

The idea that some children were not capable of being fostered also persisted, although in an attenuated form. Medical officers were no longer required to certify a child's fitness to be boarded-out, but even in 1955, instances of the successful boarding-out of 'difficult' children were sufficiently notable to be described separately in the report of the work of the Children's Department of the Home Office.[37]

Whereas, at the end of the war, about a quarter of the children in public care in England and Wales who were boarded-out were placed with relatives, this proportion fell year by year thereafter until, by the mid-1970s, it stood at about 13 per cent. It is unclear why this should have happened. There may have been a deliberate policy in that direction in some areas. Certainly after the death of Maria Colwell in 1973 (whose circumstances seemed to have been complicated by rivalries between her parents and her grandparents) some authorities became more cautious about placing children with relatives.[38] But the trend had begun its downward course before then and was only slightly accelerated afterwards. The decline may have had something to do with increasing rates of household mobility or to the higher standards being applied to the selection of foster parents in general. The phenomenon deserves to be studied. Nevertheless, the consequences were plain: more unrelated foster parents had to be found.

Understanding post-war trends in foster care

As in so much of child care history, the relationship between the different parts of the system is of the utmost importance in understanding post-war trends in foster care. For example, in 1955 it could be officially recorded that the factor that had most affected the development of children's Homes in the last few years was the appearance of the family group Home in which a small group of children, usually about 6 to 12 of varied ages, lived in a private house with a housemother whose husband went out to his usual work. At the end of 1954 there were already 400 such family group Homes. Although in total this form of provision only catered for a limited number of children, its significance was considerable in some areas. It symbolised a different and more homely form of residential care that was entirely unlike the large institutional establishments that had gone before. Indeed, the family group home with half-a-dozen children on a housing estate might be regarded as rather like a foster home that took several children. The criticism of residential care could be met and deflected without necessarily having to replace it by foster care. Thus, it can be argued that as the quality of residential care was seen to be being improved so, in some areas, the incentive to develop foster care was diminished.

There are, therefore, several factors that help to explain why, despite periods of intense encouragement from the Home Office, boarding-out did not develop as fast or as extensively as might have been expected in the 25 years after the end of the war. Further significant developments awaited new organisational, political, financial and professional environments in the 1980s.

Important amongst these have been the establishment of special fostering (and adoption) teams and the growing conviction that, given enough care and energy virtually no child was unplaceable. These developments were aided by the dissemination of ideas about good practice that was encouraged by the work of organisations like the British Agencies for Adoption and Fostering and by Barnardo's. Yet, as much as anything else, the rapidly rising cost of residential care has imparted a renewed momentum to the quest for more foster homes. As 'value for money' has become the test of successful policy, auditors and accountants have added their voices to the clamour for foster care to be expanded.[39] In this climate, the belief that the best form of care is also the cheapest has become politically irresistible.

Nevertheless, in spite of all these favourable factors only 52 per cent of the children in the care of local authorities in 1986 in England and Wales were boarded-out.[40] However, another 16 per cent were 'home on trial' with parents or relatives and, therefore, not available to be placed in foster homes although they were still in care. If this group is excluded from the calculation then the rate of foster care rises to 62 per cent. Even so, a third of all children in care still remain in residential care of one kind or another and many more than this will have experienced a residential placement sometime in their careers.[41] There still appear to be many factors that impede the development of foster care beyond a certain level, although in 1986 local rates varied from 35 per cent to 89 per cent. Nonetheless, most clustered around the mean. An analysis of that and related issues takes us beyond the history and into the sphere of current policy and practice. However, in the next chapter some of the variations that existed in the policies and practices of apparently similar child care organisations are identified and discussed.

ypical Barnardo's Boys Home (above) and Girls Home of the 1950's (below).

(Below). A group activity at one of several Day Care centres opened by Barnardo's in 1972.

ove). A nursery home of the 1930's.

"PULLS OUT OF A BASKET IN SPITALFIELDS MARKET." (*See page* 65.)

An engraving from the 1877 edition of Night & Day, a publication produced by Dr Barnardo in his efforts to raise funds. It was not possible at this time to reproduce photographs in printed form.

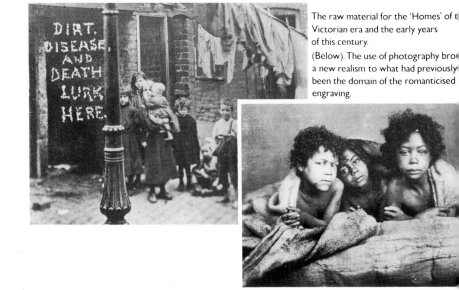

DIRT, DISEASE, AND DEATH LURK HERE.

The raw material for the 'Homes' of the Victorian era and the early years of this century.
(Below). The use of photography brought a new realism to what had previously been the domain of the romanticised engraving.

An Approved School of the 1940's. An army type regime existed with morning parades (above) and the detailing of groups of boys to work on the home farm where much of the produce used in the school was grown (below).

(Above). The majority of Boarding Out took place in rural areas where it provided a second source of income to the many families who participated in the scheme. (Below). The Boarding Out officer also carried out a physical inspection during her periodic visits.

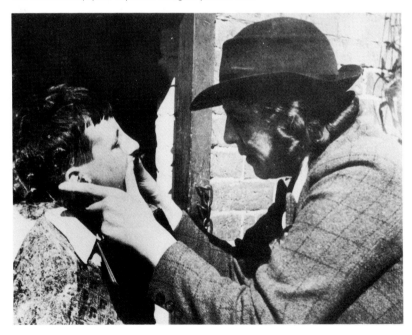

5 Comparisons and contrasts

I Similarities and differences

So far we have concentrated upon the public sector in our view of the history of foster care. The history of its development in the voluntary sector shows certain similarities but also some significant differences. The main voluntary children's organisations have been Barnardo's, the Waifs and Strays Society (renamed the Church of England Children's Society), the Methodist Children's Homes and Orphanages (later the National Children's Home) and a group of largely autonomous Catholic agencies. As we have seen, all these societies were founded or substantially developed in the 1870s and 1880s, so that they entered the field of foster care somewhat later than the poor law system.

The voluntary societies compared with the poor law system
There were several ways in which the societies differed from the poor law guardians in their organisation of boarding-out. First, it was not subject to any governmental regulation and hence there were no externally imposed restrictions upon who could or could not be boarded-out. The voluntary organisations were free to place children of any age; they did not have to obtain any certificate of 'fitness for placement' and there was no limit upon how many children they could place in any one foster home. Indeed, it is interesting to see that whereas the central government authorities gradually brought voluntary Homes under their inspection, a similar degree of regulation was never extended to foster homes in the voluntary sector. Secondly, the voluntary societies differed from the Poor Law in that until the years after the Second World War they removed children from their foster homes at certain ages to bring them back into residential care, usually in order (so it was argued) to train them in a trade. This was quite at odds with poor law policy, the whole thrust of which was to keep children from returning to the mainstream system at all costs, for fear that they would become dependent and lifelong paupers. Whereas in the public system foster care was regarded as a means of breaking the cycle of pauperism, the child in the voluntary sector was usually assumed to have made that break already simply by virtue of not being looked after by the Poor Law. Thirdly, during the inter-war period

the rates of boarding-out achieved by some of the philanthropic societies did not all fall in the way that they did in the public system. Finally, the voluntary societies were keen to board-out children in the countryside. This was in sharp contrast to the prevailing preference of boards of guardians who were usually anxious to keep children within the boundaries of their own unions.

These were important differences between Poor Law practices and those of the voluntary societies and reflected certain differences in objectives, as well as in relationships with central government. However, there were also considerable similarities. With the exception of Barnardo's, the societies had similar proportions of children in foster homes as were to be found in the Poor Law. Women inspectors were appointed under both systems and seem to have worked in much the same fashion and entertained similar doubts and anxieties as well as recording similar difficulties in recruiting satisfactory foster parents. Rates of boarding-out allowances were much the same and the undertakings that foster parents were required to sign did not differ substantially. The greatest similarity, however, was the close connection between residential care and foster care. By and large the level of foster care was determined by what was happening in the Homes, and as that varied, so the repercussions affected the fortunes of foster care.

Some of the societies even developed schemes that would have been classified by the Poor Law as out-door relief. For example, Barnardo's introduced an auxiliary boarding-out scheme whereby the Society met part of the expense incurred by unmarried mothers in placing their child privately, albeit selection was subject to close moral scrutiny. The child had to be the only child and Barnardo had to be satisfied that the mother was 'penitent and desirous of leading a better life' and employable if 'unhampered' with a child, and willing to contribute to its upkeep.[1] The scheme reached a peak of 1,000 payments just after the First World War and rose to that level again in 1941. Both the Waifs and Strays and the NCH had somewhat similar arrangements, but of a rather more informal and less systematic kind.

However, it would be misleading to concentrate solely upon the ways in which the voluntary children's societies resembled or differed from the Poor Law for there was an equally elaborate patchwork of similarities and variations amongst them. It is as hazardous to generalise about the policies of the societies as it is about those of the boards of guardians. This can be illustrated by reference to the development of boarding-out within the main organisations.

II Barnardo's and boarding-out

Barnardo's began boarding-out children in a systematic fashion in 1886. Only children who were orphans, deserted or abandoned were at first considered to be suitable, although orphanhood was often interpreted rather loosely. A medically qualified lady visitor (Jane Walker) was appointed the following year and was required to visit the children once every three months during the first year and every six months thereafter. She was joined later by other, similarly qualified, women inspectors. Local voluntary committees were set up to recruit foster parents and to help with the supervision.

The rapid expansion of Barnardo's boarding-out system

Barnardo's system developed rapidly and by 1891 a third of all the children in their care were in foster homes. Both the number and the proportion fell back somewhat during the rest of the decade largely, it has been argued, as a result of the Society's financial problems and the insistence, on the part of the trustees, that the number of admissions should be curtailed.[2] Indeed, there is some evidence that the growth of boarding-out shadowed the growth in the number of children in care and that when this ceased, the rate of boarding-out also ceased to grow or actually dropped. This suggests that, as in the Poor Law system, when the numbers in care declined, first priority was given to using the inelastic resources of the residential Homes as fully as possible. The evidence against this view is that without very much of an increase in the total number of children in Barnardo's care during the period from 1917 to 1919 there was a surge in boarding-out so that, by 1919, 48 per cent of all the children were in foster homes. This was certainly a remarkable achievement but one that is not easily explained, especially in view of the turmoil of the war years. There were two factors that may have played a part in this expansion. One was the termination of all child emigration because of the U-boat danger in the Atlantic. Instead of going to Canada, 'eligible' children were placed in foster homes in Britain. The other was the existence of a growing number of war widows who may have provided a new source of foster mothers.

Central commitment to the principle of boarding-out

Over the longer period, however, an assortment of factors combined to facilitate the growth in boarding-out within Barnardo's. First, there was the fact of a central commitment. Barnardo repeatedly emphasised the virtues of boarding-out, maintaining that its advantages were that it was

better and healthier for the child; that it was economical; that it counter-
acted the drift of the population from the countryside to the towns; and
that it helped to increase the income of working people in rural areas.
Barnardo was at pains to stress that 'institutionalism was the great danger
to avoid' and that 'children must be brought up under homely and natural
surroundings'. However, like the poor law inspectors, he recognised that
boarding-out without constant supervision was 'fraught with perilous
possibilities'.[3]

Local committees
Secondly, this central direction could be translated into action through
the activities of the local committees that had been established around
the country. This was in marked contrast to the public sector where the
central leadership was lukewarm and where the local boarding-out
committees were little used by the boards of guardians that looked upon
them from a distance with suspicion and indifference.

Size of placements
Thirdly, Barnardo's placed rather more children in each foster home than
the guardians. For instance, in her 1888 report, Walker included
information about the homes that she had visited: in about half of them
there were one or two children; in a third, three or four; and in the
remainder, five or more (the largest number being 10).

The long-term nature of most of Barnardo's boarding-out
Fourthly, many of the children admitted to Barnardo's were classified
as 'permanent' cases (80 per cent in 1910, rising to 90 per cent by 1934).
The poor law system dealt with many more short-term admissions – the
notorious 'ins and outs' as they came to be called. By contrast Barnardo's,
as well as the other voluntary societies, had a much slower turnover of
children and this lent itself to the development of the kind of long-term
arrangements that foster parents appeared to prefer. In addition, the strict
rules about visiting that Barnardo's adopted and the distances involved
made it unlikely that foster parents would be troubled by visiting parents.

Of course, relatively long-term placements meant that foster parents
could only be used for a limited number of children. However, this
problem may have been eased, deliberately or not, by the policy of
withdrawing children from their foster homes when they left school and
then returning them to a children's Home. Whether or not foster parents
were willing to take another child when this happened is unclear, although
the fact that many of them looked after several children at the same
timesuggests that they were prepared to accept a succession of youngsters.

The effects of emigration on the rate of turnover in foster homes
As well as being removed from their foster homes when they left school
(and when the boarding-out allowance ceased) many children were also
removed in order to go to Canada, typically between the ages of 10 and
12. In 1908, for instance, 28 per cent of Barnardo's emigration parties
were formed from children who had come directly from foster homes.
There are at least three possible explanations. First, June Rose has argued
that, at least in the early years, 'boarding-out was seen as a preparation
for emigration',[4] although the evidence for this as a policy is far from
conclusive. Secondly, emigration may have been used to deal with foster
home breakdowns, rather than bringing children back into residential care.
However, the statistics which are available on breakdowns do not suggest
that this was the case. Even so, removal with a view to emigration might
have disguised imminent disruptions. Thirdly, by the end of the century,
emigration had become something of a competition between the voluntary
societies and there is archival evidence that shows that special efforts
were made to swell the size of each successive emigration party.[5] A
sweep through the foster homes may have provided extra numbers.

Thus, the removal of children from their foster homes, whether to
return to a children's Home in Britain or to be sent to Canada, may have
reflected the need to secure a reasonable rate of turnover. By removing
somewhat older children from foster homes, places might be freed for
others and the number of children boarded-out thereby sustained. Indeed,
the desire for growth which Barnardo always entertained for his organisation almost certainly added to the importance of high levels of turnover
and that, as we have seen, was particularly difficult to achieve if most
of the children were admitted on a permanent basis.

No concept of an 'unfit' child for boarding-out
There is a final factor that has already been touched on which might help
to explain the more extensive development of boarding-out by Barnardo's
than by the poor law authorities. There were no hard and fast rules that
debarred certain classes of children from being placed in foster homes.
Certainly, some of the Barnardo children who were boarded-out suffered
from mental and physical handicaps that would have ruled them out for
placement had they been in the poor law system.[6] Likewise, by 1900
many babies were being boarded-out. This may have been made more
possible because the spectre of baby-farming that had hung over child
care for at least 30 years (despite the introduction of infant protection
legislation) was receding. The employment of medically qualified visitors

may have also gone some way towards counteracting the criticisms that too many risks attached to the boarding-out of babies and the handicapped.

The maintenance of the rate of boarding-out by Barnardo's

Unlike the public care sector, there was no diminution in the rate of boarding-out by Barnardo's in the inter-war years. Indeed, a high rate (compared with other agencies) of about 45 per cent was maintained throughout most of these years. We have already noted that a striking feature of the work of the voluntary societies during this period was the lack of change. They seemed to be engulfed by the weight of earlier tradition and unable or unwilling to break free. Until the upheavals of the Second World War, there were few external forces that required them to alter either their policies or their practices. By contrast, we have seen that a major transformation occurred in the organisation of public child care in 1930. Alongside this, substantial changes were made in the social security system that, by the second half of the 1930s, had begun to weaken the hitherto close links between public cash assistance and public care. The first of these changes allowed a start to be made with the reform of residential care whilst the second tended to reduce the number of children coming into public care because of their parents' poverty. Both factors lessened the need for the public assistance authorities to develop foster care. These changes hardly seem to have disturbed the established practices of Barnardo's. The number of children placed in the Homes was kept at much the same level; applications for admission remained similar to those before the war, as did the proportion that was accepted. As a result the number of children in care stayed fairly constant throughout the 1920s and '30s. There were no pressing reasons either to enlarge or diminish the use of foster care. For example, the practice of recalling foster children to a branch Home at 14 continued until after the Second World War.

During and after the war, the rate of fostering in Barnardo's was maintained at about the same level, although this was to some extent achieved because the number in foster homes fell less than the total number of children in their care. Nevertheless, foster care remained a prominent feature of Barnardo's work even though the decision soon after the war to promote adoption meant that certain long-term foster children passed out of the Society's care. However, on the other hand, the decision, at about the same time, to end the practice of removing children from foster homes when they left school naturally added to the numbers in those homes.

The voluntary children's societies in the post-war period

The last 40 years of the history of the children's societies have witnessed dramatic changes of which Barnardo's has been a part. Year by year there has been a reduction in the number of children cared for by the voluntary sector: from nearly 29,000 in 1949 to 4,000 in 1984.[7] The creation of local authority children's departments, separate from public assistance and with an increasing number of trained staff, had improved the image and acceptability of the public sector. The changes in the community homes system after the 1969 Children and Young Persons Act increased the dependence of the voluntary societies upon the local authority system, both for referrals and for support. Soon after, the emergence of social services departments and the reform of local government led to the local authorities becoming larger and more self-sufficient. Although the proportion of children looked after by the voluntary societies who were in the care of local authorities rose (from 13 per cent in 1949 to 84 per cent in 1984) their number fell steadily, contributing to the continuing decline in the total for whom the societies were responsible.

In the post-war period Barnardo's was the only voluntary society to sustain a substantial level of boarding-out. Its residential Homes, though important, therefore played a smaller part in its total activities than was the case in other societies. That seems to have made it somewhat easier to develop a variety of community-based services as attitudes towards residential care became less favourable and as costs rose. Those societies that had continued to rely heavily upon their Homes seem to have found that shift harder to make.

III   Other voluntary societies and boarding-out

The Waifs and Strays Society

The Waifs and Strays Society (now the Children's Society) which was founded in 1881 organised and used foster homes from the outset. By the turn of the century they too were boarding-out about a quarter of all the children in their care, although in absolute terms the number was much smaller than Barnardo's. However, there were important differences. In particular, they tended to place proportionately more boys than girls in foster homes, almost certainly because more residential places were provided exclusively for girls because of the Society's particular involvement with rescue from (or from the risk of) prostitution.

In most of the other societies, as well as within the Poor Law, girls in care were more likely to be placed in foster homes than boys, a

difference that persists to the present. Historically, there were several
reasons for this. In many cases boarding-out was developed for girls
because it was considered to provide a better preparation than a Home
for a future as servants, wives and mothers. Residential Homes were
unlikely, it was often claimed, to instil the necessary domestic skills and
virtues. They were, in any case, 'worse for girls than boys, because girls
are especially dependent upon the affections'.[8] The growing influence
of women within the Poor Law and within the voluntary sector added
a particular force to the criticism of institutional care for girls. For example,
Jane Senior, the first woman central government inspector appointed by
the Local Government Board in 1873, prepared a scathing report on the
education of girls in poor law schools.[9] Underlying her attack and her
advocacy of boarding-out was the view (shared by other women like her)
that women and girls should not be 'overseen' by men. Deprived and
destitute females needed to be dealt with by other women, albeit of a
superior class. Boarding-out fitted in well with such aspirations, for
placements could be selected and supervised by committees of ladies
(outside the excessive influence of predominantly male boards of
guardians) and the day-to-day care and instruction of the girls would be
largely in the hands of respectable wives and mothers.

There were, therefore, important factors connected with the demand
for good domestic servants and an emerging 'women's view' that
contributed to there being a greater proportion of girls than boys in foster
homes. There was also the frequently recorded fact that those who came
forward to offer their services as foster parents more often sought girls
than boys. This may well have been a reflection of their greater usefulness
in helping in the home, as well as of the belief that they were easier to
manage and less troublesome. A deeper study of the differential use of
foster care for girls and boys would provide an interesting insight into
prevailing images of femininity and masculinity.

General policies on boarding-out
The particular concern with the care of sexually wayward girls that the
Waifs and Strays developed led them to the conclusion that such girls
could not (and should not) be boarded-out and that special residential
provision was needed. These were older girls who, it was considered,
were unfit to go to ordinary households as either foster children or
domestic servants, at least until they had undergone considerable retraining and, in some cases, treatment for venereal disease. Sexually
promiscuous boys were not subjects for rescue; few were, therefore, ruled
out for foster care on those grounds.

The Waifs and Strays did, however, adopt a general rule that all children under 7 years of age should be placed with foster parents, although recent work by Harriet Ward indicates that this objective was not realised in practice.[10] For example, she has found that in the period 1887-94 only about two in five of all children under 7 were boarded-out upon admission. The Society also operated a general policy that, unless there were special circumstances, children over the age of 7 should not be boarded-out and never later than 10 years of age. Notwithstanding these restrictions, the Waifs and Strays Society did not remove older foster children in order to bring them back into residential care as was common practice in the other voluntary organisations.

Despite some of these differences the Waifs and Strays Society saw the advantages of boarding-out in much the same light as Barnardo. For example, Rudolf, the Society's secretary, explained to the Mundella Committee in 1896 that boarding-out was such a good system because:

> 'it is economical; it provides a real home, and very often a mother's love – which a child can never get in an institution . . . the opportunities that boarded-out children have of becoming acquainted with domestic service are greater than they would be in an institution; they have to assist the foster parent in many details of household work, and are thus daily prepared for after-life. . . .'[11]

Nevertheless, the rate of boarding-out achieved by the Waifs and Strays Society gradually dropped from its peak just before the turn of the century but began to rise again by the 1930s, reaching the same level in 1939 as had prevailed in 1899. Again, the story is of little if any development in boarding-out in the inter-war years. We have already considered some of the general reasons for this phenomenon but in the case of the Waifs and Strays Society, at least one other factor may need to be taken into account.

The assimilation of small organisations by the main voluntary societies
Part of the flow of children into the care of the principal voluntary child care organisations resulted from their acquisition of small private Homes or small organisations that, for one reason or another chose not to continue independently. This process of incorporation had two implications for the extent to which boarding-out was used. First, because it involved taking over institutions as well as children it increased the residential resources that, unless sold off, were available to be used. Furthermore, since many of the small enterprises had been run down before transfer,

the larger organisations often acquired more residential places than children. Secondly, some of these institutions were rather specialised in nature: industrial schools; homes for 'friendless girls'; training homes for young servants; emigration homes; ship schools; and so on. Many of the resident children would not have been regarded as suitable for boarding-out – especially the older ones.

So, it is important to appreciate that the assimilation of other small organisations was one factor that determined the number of children looked after by the main voluntary societies – and that this was associated with the transfer of institutions. This may well have retarded the development of boarding-out, especially in societies such as the Waifs and Strays.[12]

The National Children's Home

Other children's societies appear to have been rather less enthusiastic about boarding-out than Barnardo's and the Waifs and Strays. The annual reports of the Methodist National Children's Home (formerly Children's Home and Orphanages and headed by T. B. Stephenson until his retirement in 1901) make no reference to the subject until 1908. However, in that year it was noted that the Society had been boarding-out children in foster homes since the late 1880s.[13]

Despite a sluggish start, the NCH was boarding-out almost a quarter of its children in 1909. The general impetus may well have been similar to that in Birmingham where, in 1905, the principal of a Home received permission, because of its 'congested condition', to board-out 10 of the smaller children.[14] However, that factor seems to have been insufficient to maintain the peak rate of boarding-out achieved in 1909, for this was not reached again until 1930, after which there was a rapid decline in the use of foster care until, by 1939, only about 200 (or 7 per cent) of the children in the Society's care were with foster parents.

The policy of recall of boarded-out children

The strong missionary flavour of the work of Stephenson's organisation may account for the particular emphasis placed upon residential care. In the Homes, children would live in a religious atmosphere and in a community within which missionary workers could be trained. This is how that aspect was described in 1900:

> 'The child needs the education of a well ordered community; he needs the discipline of school, the workshop, and the drill ground. He needs to be part of a system which will draw forth all his

faculties, which will follow him as he goes into life, and guide and guard him through his dangerous youth, and which will be a polar point around which his thoughts and memories will revolve all his life.'[15]

We have seen that Barnardo's called back boarded-out children to their Homes when they left school. The NCH's policy on this was more stringent. The rule was that 'they should come into one of the Branches of the Home when 7 or 8 years of age'.[16] Nevertheless, some foster parents, it was reported, became so attached to the children that they 'adopted' them rather than be parted.[17] Certainly, the NCH recorded a steady trickle of 'adoptions' from the earliest years of its activity; by 1920 there had been some 260.[18] No clue is to be found among its various publications as to why the recall policy was imposed at such young ages. One might speculate that it was connected with the desire to retain a firm missionary control over the children's development during their most formative years. Yet such an explanation sits somewhat uneasily with the steady emigration of children which the NCH also organised from 1873 onwards. From then until 1915 over 2,500 left for Canada. However, they were usually children of 12 or 13, by which time it may have been assumed that their faith was well founded and secure.

Given the persistence of the recall policy it is obviously vital to trace the changing age structure of the children in the care of organisations like the NCH if a proper account is to be provided of the ups and downs in the use of foster care. Unfortunately detailed information about ages is not systematically available but it seems possible that the marked fall in the number and proportion of children who were boarded-out by the NCH in the 1930s, and indeed after the war (it was just 3 per cent in 1946), owed a good deal to there being more older children to be looked after.

The effects of the number in care
There is also the issue of the total number in care. During the 1930s the NCH looked after some 3,000 children by comparison with 4,500 in the Waifs and Strays and 8,000 in Barnardo's. The greater the number of children in care, the greater the use of foster care would seem to have been. That certainly applied to many of the small societies; they boarded-out few if any children at all. Their centre of operations was the local (and often the *only*) children's Home.

Likewise, to the extent that the local branches of the national societies revolved around a particular Home, it became the focal point of energies and loyalties; indeed such Homes provided the societies with their local identity. The smaller the society, the more likely it was that a single local Home would fulfil this function and thereby discourage initiatives to develop foster care – especially if it were seen as an alternative rather than a supplement.

This was all the more so where the homes were designed along cottage lines, with each cottage run by a 'homely foster mother', for then the criticism of bleak institutionalism could be refuted and the distinction between residential care and foster care played down. Indeed, this was an argument that Stevenson had used from the early days of the NCH and which was still deployed years later, in defence of the Society's reliance upon its Homes.

The Catholic child care organisations

The Catholic child care organisations provide a quite different story from the others with respect to boarding-out. First, Catholic child care provision was mainly based in the dioceses and archdioceses. Each operated in a substantially autonomous fashion and hence it is not easy to obtain an overall picture. But for the 13 dioceses for which information is available from 1914, it is plain that the number of children in care rose to a peak of some 15,000 in 1916 and then settled at about the 10,000 mark from the early 1920s until the early post-war years.[19]

However, there is little evidence of anything more than a handful of children being boarded-out. For example, none were recorded by the large Westminster diocese from 1911 to 1924, although there had been some throughout the 1880s and 1890s. Despite the lack of detailed information it is probably reasonable to conclude that boarding-out by the Catholic diocesan authorities was virtually non-existent until at least the 1950s. However, the picture is complicated by the existence of a separate Crusade of Rescue Society. For most years, from the turn of the century until 1939, there were between 500 and 900 children being cared for by the Crusade and of these between 10 and 20 per cent were boarded-out. However, the system was operated as a means of caring for babies. By the age of 5 and often earlier, infants were brought back into the residential Homes. The regulations attaching to foster care were both detailed and apparently stringent. For example, children were visited fortnightly and there was a special visit once a month 'when the child is stripped and weighed'.[20] Children were 'promptly withdrawn' if the regulations were not properly observed. Moreover, according to an account written in 1911:

'the receipt of poor relief, the unemployment of the husband, signs of interference, or any circumstances by which the child would suffer loss or be endangered, is sufficient to remove the home from the approved list.'

Schedules specified for every age from 1 month to 5 years, 'the kind of food, the times of feeding . . . and precise instruction as to light and sunshine, fresh air, clothing and washing'.[21]

Factors affecting the use of foster care by Catholic agencies

Clearly, foster care was regarded as hazardous and needing close supervision and regulation. However, that is not enough to explain its very limited use by Catholic agencies. At least four other factors have to be considered. First, there was the question of the supply of suitable foster homes. Catholics tended to have larger families and, therefore, less space for extra children. They tended to be poor and poorly housed and, in some areas, enmeshed in the casual labour market, especially as new immigrants. Many lived in crowded urban areas rather than the rural communities generally favoured for foster care.

The second factor that needs to be taken into account is the relationship between the Catholic child care agencies and the Poor Law that we have already mentioned. Because of the considerable difficulty that the Catholic Church experienced in ensuring a Catholic upbringing for Catholic children within the Poor Law, they were at pains to see as many as possible transferred to Catholic institutions where their faith could be protected and preserved. As a result there was always a high proportion of poor law children in Catholic children's Homes. The importance for boarding-out of the rates of poor law children in the care of voluntary agencies lies in the fact that it was the Homes of the societies that were certified for the reception of poor law children, not foster homes. It is not entirely clear what the legal position was, but the voluntary societies at least acted as if the poor law children in their care were lesser candidates for placement in foster homes.

The third factor to be borne in mind in endeavouring to explain the low rate of use of foster homes by Catholic societies is the nature and character of their residential Homes. Many of them were run by religious Orders where the idea of communal life was strongly established, and where some of the children, especially the girls, might be expected to enter the Order when they were older. Children would tend to be absorbed into these rather disciplined and contained cultures and that may well have militated against the development of boarding-out. Similarly, the fact that major resources were located in such residential settings would certainly have encouraged their fullest use.

Finally, as we saw in Chapter 3, the voluntary societies ran almost all the reformatory and industrial schools and, to a lesser extent, their successors the approved schools. Although it was not prohibited (and by the 1930s began to be encouraged) very few children committed by the courts to industrial schools were boarded-out from these institutions. By contrast with Barnardo's, who only ran approved schools after the Second World War, the Catholic child care agencies established from the start a considerable number of reformatory and industrial schools. Hence, a larger proportion of the children in their care may well not have been regarded as eligible or suitable for foster care, especially as this would have ended the *per capita* fees that were available from the Home Office before 1919, and may have affected the general grants thereafter.

In conclusion

The issues that have been considered in this chapter, therefore, serve to illustrate certain common factors that have influenced child care developments in both the public and voluntary sectors. It has also shown that, in matters of detail, there have been considerable differences, not least amongst the various voluntary societies. However, these differences in detail have exercised a considerable long-term influence on the patterns of care that the principal agencies have made available.

Even so, they shared a marked reluctance to work towards the restoration of children with their families or, more fundamentally, to engage in work that might prevent children having to come into their care. In the final chapter we consider how and why these two aspects gradually came to form a major part of modern child care policy.

6 Modern themes

I Restoration

As we have seen, child care has a long history of separation and severance. Apart from certain features of poor law practice there are few examples, up to the Second World War, of any of the organisations working systematically to restore children to their parents. Once in care they tended to stay, unless parents took active steps to recover them. Reporting on their discussions with staff in public assistance Homes the Curtis Committee, for instance, concluded in 1946 that it was generally assumed 'that the children had been deserted and that in most cases the parents had proved themselves unworthy of guardianship'.[1] With respect to the voluntary sector, they found that only a few Homes 'made any attempt to prepare the family for the child's return or, where no interest was volunteered, to find relatives who might take an interest'.[2] Despite such observations, the Committee was not led to make any specific recommendations about the steps that might be taken to rehabilitate children with their families. By contrast, the Clyde committee in Scotland suggested that there should be 'every encouragement to . . . a reunion of the family if the parents are satisfactory'.[3]

As with setting the upper age for children to be in care at 18 rather than 16 as proposed by the Curtis Committee, the government followed the lead from Scotland on this matter and in the 1948 Children Act, a duty was placed upon local authorities 'in all cases where it appears to them consistent with the welfare of the child' to ensure that the care was taken over by a parent, guardian, relative or friend.[4] However, it must be noted that this injunction referred only to children who had been admitted to care on a voluntary basis; it did not extend to children who had been committed to the care of a local authority by a court under the provisions of the 1933 Act. Nor did it extend to children for whom the voluntary societies were wholly responsible. Indeed, this was a particular point of criticism levelled at the new legislation by Beveridge in the House of Lords where the Bill was introduced. 'There are', he pointed out, 'voluntary organisations which are based upon the principle of breaking completely all contact between the mother and child'. He felt that that was 'a dreadful thing' which the new Act would still permit.[5]

Some pro-restoration influences

Economic pressures

There were several influences that led to the prominent position accorded
to restoration in the public sphere of child care after the war. The first
was that throughout its history the Poor Law had encouraged guardians
to keep expenditure to a minimum by having the charge of a child taken
over, wherever possible, by a parent or relative. However, that
requirement was couched in terms of the need to avoid the payment of
unnecessary relief. In the 1948 formulation, the local authority had to
assure itself that restoration was consistent with a child's welfare. That
might have been a formula for rather limited engagement in rehabilitation.
This, however, was obviously not the intention. The new policy was
summed up by the Home Office as follows:

> 'Section 1(3) of the Children Act . . . gives expression to the
> conviction that the right place for a child is his own home, wherever
> possible. Local authorities are concerned to fulfil this duty, first,
> in the interests of children, secondly, because there is no justification
> for retaining in public care, and at public expense, children who
> can be provided for suitably by their parents, and, next, because
> some parents become less eager to resume responsibility for their
> children the longer the children remain in care.'[6]

Despite the emphasis upon the needs of the child, shades of poor law
thinking were still detectable and, of course, parents continued to be
financially liable to meet at least part of the cost of their children being
in care.

Evacuation

The inclusion of the restoration clause was also prompted by war-time
evacuation or, more precisely, by the fear that a substantial minority of
children in the reception areas would be abandoned by their parents at
the end of the war and would, therefore, need to be looked after on a
permanent basis by public welfare agencies unless steps were taken to
ensure that they returned home. Estimates of the number of such children
were put as high as 25,000. As it happened there were only some 1,500,
but that was not to become clear until the framing of the legislation was
well under way.[7]

Evacuation played its part in another way as well. It lent considerable
support to the growing body of research which pointed to the distress

that could be caused to young children by separation from their mothers. The 'maternal deprivation' thesis, which became more widely articulated in the 1940s, indicated that if young children had to be away from their mothers, then the shorter that period was the better.[8]

New children's departments with trained staff
The importance accorded to the aim of restoration in 1948 was also influenced by the expectation that it would become increasingly possible to achieve as the new children's departments became established and as more trained child care officers were recruited to work in the field. In the event it came to be acknowledged that such work could:

> 'occupy a great deal of effort which, when there is a shortage of child care officers, it is not easy to divert from other aspects of child care.'[9]

Certainly, whether or not steps were taken to get children back to their families depended upon the pressure of other priorities associated with reception into care and finding and supervising foster homes. It will be recalled, for instance, that training for child care was launched in 1947 as 'training for boarding-out visitors'.[10] However, the priority attached to rehabilitation also depended, to some extent, upon what had to be done to effect it. In the early post-war years, and continuing into the 1950s, there were grave housing shortages and a still large privately-rented housing sector. A substantial minority of children came into care on a voluntary basis because their parents had lost their accommodation through eviction (often by private landlords and for rent arrears) or because they had been unable to obtain accommodation and had been forced to share (usually with their parents) in overcrowded conditions. The stresses and strains inherent in such situations were liable to create disputes that degenerated to the point where young families were obliged to leave. Even by 1963, when the worst of the post-war housing crisis was over, 11 per cent of all voluntary admissions to local authority care were attributed to housing problems.[11] Unfortunately, similar data for earlier years are not available but it is reasonable to assume that the incidence was higher.

It is against this background of acute post-war housing difficulties and the decline in council house building from the mid-1950s until the incoming Labour government's renewed housing drive in the second half of the 1960s, that the character of much of the early work of rehabilitation has to be seen. Getting families rehoused loomed large in the process of enabling them to resume the care of their children. There were negotiations to be conducted with local authority housing departments to try to get the families of children in care accorded higher priorities, as well as discussion with doctors to obtain priority on medical grounds. Similar kinds of involvements were necessary with social security offices and with the public utilities about help with the payment of rent or the management of debts that had led to supplies of gas or electricity being disconnected.

Although time-consuming and frustrating, this was straightforward work inasmuch as it aimed at the resolution or amelioration of problems that were caused largely by severe housing shortages and by poverty. Even so, it was a far cry from the work of the boarding-out officers who had been the original model for what the new generation of child care officers should be and do.

'Home on trial' placements

In most of these cases the question of risk to the children in returning to their parents was not an issue. Matters were different, however, when it came to children who had been committed to care because they were judged to be in need of care or protection. Until 1956, children who were in care on these grounds could not be returned to their parents or relatives prior to the expiry of the order when they reached 18 or unless it was revoked earlier by a court. However, under the Family Allowances and National Insurance Act of that year, local authorities were permitted to place a child with parents, relatives or friends for a trial period, with the aim of preparing the ground for an application for the revocation of the order if all went well. It is not clear exactly why this important step in restoration policy should have been taken at that point. There had been a prior (but unsuccessful) private members' bill and some children's officers had already adopted the practice but had then been faced with the issue of whether or not the families were entitled to resume drawing the family allowance (hence the location of this measure in family allowance legislation).

Whatever the reasons for the change in 1956 it clarified both that local authorities were able to make such 'home on trial' placements and that, although the child remained legally 'in care', the parents could claim the family allowance for them. Thus the Act initiated one of the most important (as well as one of the most controversial) facets of restoration policy. It was to become especially significant because committed children had usually remained in care for long periods, as comparatively few orders were revoked (about 650 in 1950, for example and some 1,500 in 1954 – 4 per cent and 8 per cent respectively of the outstanding orders.[12] By contrast, large numbers of the voluntary admissions went home quickly, once short-term crises (like home confinements – which were still more common than hospital confinements in the 1950s) had passed. However, the proportion of such short-term voluntary cases began to fall and the proportion of children subject to fit person orders to rise. If substantial numbers of children were to be rehabilitated then more committed children had to go home. Furthermore, a large minority of children who had been admitted to care on a voluntary basis were subject to parental rights resolutions (the Poor Law adoptions of 1889) – there were 19 per cent in 1950 and 23 per cent by 1960. As with the committed children, these resolutions had to be rescinded if the child was to go home before they were 18. 'Home on trial' arrangements, therefore, also recommended themselves for this group as a prelude to such a step being taken. By comparison with the 1920s and '30s there were now more 'detained' children to be returned home if a policy of restoration was to be pursued and expanded; but this accentuated the need to exercise judgement about the risks that might then be entailed.

By 1960 there were 2,000 children placed 'home on trial', or about 10 per cent of all those in care subject to fit person orders. This number rose rapidly in the next year or so until, by 1970, there were over 11,000 or about 24 per cent of the committed children.[13] Of course, not all these children had been committed to care because they had been neglected or abused. Many had been placed in care because they had not attended school or because they had offended. Surprisingly, however, the number of fit person orders that were revoked fell during this period and it was not until 1969 that the 1954 level was reached again. Either steps to revoke the orders were going by default, or local authorities were anxious to have them continue because they wished to retain a measure of control despite the child having been returned to its parents.

After 1971, in the wake of the 1969 Children and Young Persons Act, all the children in the approved school system (12,300 of them) were transferred to the care of the new social services departments. As a result, the recorded number of children 'in care' was instantly swollen, both by those who were resident in the schools and by those who had been released on licence under supervision (4,800 in all). These were to count as children 'home on trial'. Over and above this, however, the use of 'home on trial' continued to grow, in absolute numbers and as a proportion, to a peak of nearly 19,000 and 27 per cent in 1978. Since then the number has steadily declined as a result of falling numbers in care but, even in 1986, 22 per cent of committed children were living with parents or relatives 'on trial'.

Factors encouraging 'home on trial'

There have been several reasons for this remarkable trend that has transformed the shape of child care in the last 20 years. The philosophy that the children's interests were best served if they could be with their families was, of course, of fundamental importance and a reaction to the damage that many children were known to have suffered through earlier policies of severance. However, restoration also reduced costs (children 'home on trial' but 'in care' cost only the salaries of the visiting social workers), not only by reducing the number of children to be looked after but also by enabling increasingly expensive residential facilities to be closed. There is, for example, evidence which indicates that the closure of many community homes with education (the former approved schools) was achieved not by placing the children in foster homes, or discharging them from care, but by returning them 'home on trial'.[14] As pressures on public expenditure mounted the economic arguments for the pursuit of policies that reduced the number of children in care became more conclusive.

Another important influence on the emergence of restoration policies has been the growing appreciation that when they eventually left care, even after long periods, most children (at least for a time) went back to their families. It is hard to know exactly how many, but from what published statistics there are it appears that, year by year, no less than 85 per cent of children return to a parent or relative when they leave care. If so many children were going home anyway it seemed reasonable to consider whether at least some of them could not return earlier and more smoothly, assisted by the preparatory work that social workers might be able to provide. Indeed, more care resources came to be designed specifically for short-term use (like short-term specialist foster care) with the clear expectation and intention that children should be swiftly restored to their families.

Child care research

However, important though policies of restoration have been, especially as radical departures from the legacy of severance, they have been neither fully implemented nor received unequivocal support. Clearly, not all the children who might have been restored to their parents were being restored, or at least not with the active encouragement of social workers. The issue was forcefully exposed in 1973 when Rowe and Lambert published the results of their research in a book entitled *Children Who Wait*.[15] The study told a sorry story of many children languishing in care for the want of deliberate plans either for them to go home or, if this was not possible, for them to be found permanent alternative families. The influence of the book was far-reaching, causing many social services departments to review how they planned for the children in their care.[16]

In terms of rehabilitation one of the major problems appeared to be the erosion of contact between the child in care and their parents and relatives. Other studies also made it clear that the processes whereby these links were weakened began early in a child's care career: the longer they stayed in care, the greater the likelihood that they would not be restored to their parents.[17] Little child care research was undertaken before the 1960s, but in the 1970s, more began to be done and of a kind that exercised an influence on the issues appearing on the political agenda. Priorities began to be modified so that more time and other resources were devoted to working with the families of children in care.

Growth in the number in care during the 1970s

Alongside the influence of research there was a remarkable growth in the number of children in care during most of the 1970s. Part of this increase was accounted for by the transfer of approved school children to social services departments in 1971; but the growth continued, to reach an all-time peak of 101,000 in 1977. This was particularly disturbing because it was a 'real' growth; that is, not one attributable to an increase in the overall size of the child population.[18] However, during the same period the number of children coming into care each year was falling. Obviously, children were staying in care longer, and although much of this reflected a sharp rise in the number who were being committed to care (from 10 per cent of the total in 1968 to 30 per cent in 1978) it still suggested that not enough was being done to restore children to their families as soon as possible.[19]

The reasons for the pronounced rise in the number of children in care in England and Wales in the 1970s were complicated and, even now, are not fully understood. At the time there appeared to be no sign that the trend would be halted or reversed. Pressure on the services mounted, as did expenditure. Steps were called for in order to check the apparently relentless upward spiral. Moves to prevent children coming into care received renewed encouragement as did various strategies (like 'home on trial') that led to children being discharged from care more quickly. Restoration was squarely on the agenda; and this contributed to the dramatic fall in the number of children in care that has occurred in the 1980s (a 30 per cent reduction in the period 1978 to 1986).

However, the coincidence of economic and professional factors in stimulating the development of these policies was also supplemented by a disquiet that children were being taken into care unnecessarily and precipitately (for instance, through such procedures as the use of emergency place of safety orders). That disquiet found public expression in various ways, not least through the activities of bodies like the Family Rights Group.

Yet such pressure, together with the earlier return home of children (especially those who had been neglected or abused), exposed more clearly than at any time in child care history the tension between the two aspirations of child protection and child restoration. The tension had been detectable within the Poor Law, but to all intents and purposes was suppressed in the voluntary movement by the overriding priority that had been accorded to child-saving and child control. By the 1970s, and even more during the 1980s, the contradiction that this tension reflected posed a profound dilemma for those charged with the responsibility of deciding whether or not it was best for certain children to stay with, or be returned to their parents.[20] A series of tragic deaths, such as that of Jasmine Beckford in 1985, served to accentuate the dilemma and to place it in the limelight of public scrutiny.[21] The contending objectives have been even more vividly highlighted by the growing concern with the sexual abuse of children, as the Cleveland Report has demonstrated.[22]

The acute modern child care dilemma

The conviction and self-confidence of the 19th century child-savers have been replaced by the doubts and uncertainties of the latter part of the 20th. Once the justification for severance came to be questioned, it was only a matter of time before a fundamental dilemma in child care policy and practice became agonisingly apparent.

This dilemma manifested itself in many ways, not least in resistance to restoration. It was too easy for parents to recover their children when this jeopardised their welfare: we had gone too far. Evidence of this view was to be found in the provision included in the 1975 Children Act whereby, after a child who had been admitted to care on a voluntary basis had been in care for six months, parents were required to give 28 days notice before they could lawfully have him back.[23] A number of speakers in the parliamentary debate on the 1948 Children Bill had pressed for such a clause, but without success. By the 1970s the climate had changed and the protection of children from disruption, as well as from neglect and abuse, had become matters of more pressing concern. The 1975 legislation also reflected that change in the new measures that it introduced in order to make it easier for children in care who were considered unlikely ever to return to their own family, to be adopted .[24]

It was not, however, only in connection with the protection of children that the conflict between separation and restoration became so evident. Magistrates had been unhappy since the 1969 Children and Young Persons Act that they no longer had the power, in making a care order with respect to a juvenile offender, to ensure that the child was removed from home and detained for a minimum period as had been possible when approved school orders were available. If they made one of the new orders the local authority to whose care the child was committed had the right to send that child home at any time without reference to the court or, indeed, to allow him to remain at home from the outset. In the view of many magistrates, social services departments erred on the side of restoration and in doing so were frustrating what had been intended by the court.[25] Eventually, in 1982, the magistrates won a concession. Under certain circumstances they were to be allowed to add a residence condition to a care order which effectively prevented a young offender being able to return home earlier than a court had in mind.[26] However, soon after this legislation was in place the issue subsided, largely because fewer juvenile delinquents were being made subject to care orders: few residence conditions have been made.

There was no such relaxation in the confrontation between the need to protect children from abusive or otherwise unfit parents and the need for children to be with their natural parents whenever possible. Indeed, the tension between the two objectives intensified. It is far from clear where, in any particular case, the best interests of the child lie. Indeed, it was to try to obtain a better assessment of these matters that provision was made in the 1975 Children Act for the separate representation of children in care proceedings and for the appointment of a *guardian ad litem* 'for the purposes of the proceeding'.[27] It was not to be assumed automatically that the interests of the child and those of the parents were compatible and, therefore, it was not to be assumed that the parent could – or should – represent the child.

The problem that these measures address is not new. What is new (at least in historical terms) is the emergence of politically powerful economic, professional and civil rights ideologies that each stress (albeit for somewhat different reasons) the desirability of not separating children from their parents. These now stand in opposition to an equally powerful and long-standing ideology (augmented by other aspects of civil rights thinking) that emphasises the duty to protect children from unfit parents and, in doing so, to ensure that as little disruption as possible occurs thereafter. This is the theme of the last section of this chapter. First, however, we look at the history, since 1948, of the idea and practice of prevention.

II Prevention

Commentaries on the role of prevention in the development of child care policies are apt to date its emergence from the 1963 Children and Young Persons Act because, for the first time, local authorities were authorised to spend money on forestalling the appearance of children before a court or on avoiding their having to be received into care. These provisions also included permission to provide assistance in cash if this were considered to be necessary to achieve these ends. However, as Jean Packman has pointed out, there had already been a considerable growth in preventive activities in a number of children's departments well before the 1963 Act.[28] Indeed, it had been seven years since the Ingleby Committee was first asked to include in its review of the law relating to juvenile delinquents an examination of whether local authorities should be given new powers and duties 'to prevent or forestall the suffering of children through neglect in their own homes'.[29]

Differing definitions of the concept of prevention
The legislation of 1963 is, therefore, a rather misleading landmark in the history of prevention in child care, not least because the principle of prevention, as we have seen, had been invoked from the earliest days of organised child care. The voluntary societies were anxious, through separation, to prevent children from being exposed to squalor, crime and sinfulness and from returning to vicious or neglectful parents. Likewise, the Poor Law was always concerned to prevent children from staying in care unnecessarily or from growing up to become the next generation of paupers. Over and above this, a guiding force within the Poor Law was, of course, the conviction that people had to be deterred (that is, prevented) from resorting to relief. What changed after 1948 was what it was considered necessary and feasible to prevent – namely the disruption or breakdown of families that led to children having to be looked after by a corporate body.[30] This interpretation of prevention entailed major changes in the orientation of most care services. Traditionally, they had been organised to provide substitute care not to work directly with families. Nor had they operated in local communities in order to contrive solutions to family problems through the mobilisation of an assortment

of resources which were not in their immediate control. There were, of course, exceptions. From the start, the NSPCC worked with families and did not establish Homes or recruit foster parents of its own. Indeed, it was both significant and remarkable that in the 1880s it incorporated the word 'prevention' in its title. There were also other general family welfare organisations (such as the Family Welfare Association and the Family Service Units) that adopted the same approach. Looking at these differences it could be argued that the principal impediment to the wider development of prevention as it is understood today was the existence of extensive facilities for providing substitute care for children, especially the residential Homes.

Factors hampering the development of modern prevention policies
However, there were other factors that hampered the shift towards the modern conception of prevention. First, such a transformation implied confidence in the ability of parents to manage if they were given enough help at the right time. It required an alteration in the basic assumptions about the causes of social ills. Parents (as well as children) could not continue to be regarded as the irredeemable perpetrators of their own plight. Instead, they had to be seen as largely the victims of their circumstances. The implications of this could be far-reaching if the amelioration of those circumstances began to be taken seriously. As in the sphere of public health, effective prevention could not be achieved entirely on an individual basis. But, to the extent that it was concerned with the effects of poverty – and therefore inequality – it harboured the seeds of a radical ideology that threatened to disturb prevailing social and economic arrangements. Inevitably, once the prevention of the reception of children into care suggested that more than individual first aid was required, its development was liable to be checked, ostensibly on the grounds of its cost but, more fundamentally, on the grounds of its disturbing logic.

A second general factor that has impeded the development of prevention in child care is the politics of organisational collaboration. Once families began to be helped with the problems that threatened disruption and collapse it was but a short step to the realisation that these problems did not fit neatly into the remit of any single social service agency. Prevention called for help on several fronts which, if it were to be both effective and efficient, needed to be co-ordinated. Both nationally and locally this proved to be far from easy as departments and organisations jockeyed for the lead role or reacted defensively to initiatives that appeared to threaten their domain. Lacking a clear superordinate authority, the informal systems of co-ordination that were developed were found to be inordinately difficult to work. Different agencies were exposed to different pressures and had different priorities.[31] Early initiatives in preventive collaboration (such as the local co-ordinating committees suggested by the Home Office, Ministry of Health and Ministry of Education joint circular in 1950[32]) were rarely a match for these political problems. Organisational bargaining and negotiation tended to have to be conducted on each case afresh rather than being settled at a policy level. Duplication came to be criticised as often as the failure to provide any assistance at all.

The 1963 Act helped to reduce some of these problems for it placed a duty upon every local authority 'to make available such advice, guidance and assistance as may promote the welfare of children by diminishing the need to receive . . . or keep them in care'[33] but it left unresolved the question of how co-ordination was to be achieved amongst the many bodies that could be involved with families that were confronted by a bewildering array of problems. It was partly to resolve such issues that the Seebohm Committee recommended in 1968 that the scattered welfare responsibilities of local authorities should be integrated into a single social services department and that there should also be integration at the central level.[34] These recommendations were adopted in the Local Authority Social Services Act, 1970. Even so, there remained (and remains) considerable difficulty in co-ordinating the mixture of action that prevention requires. Co-ordination imposes its own costs (not least in the time spent in meetings) which not everyone is equally willing to incur. By contrast to the simple 'preventive' solution of removing a child from its home, measures to avoid that happening are complicated, not only by the nature of the problems but by the undertones of political, administrative and economic dissent. These complexities have undoubtedly hampered the progress of prevention in child care.

There is, however, a third reason for its tardy development, and that has been its potential scale. As the cause of prevention became more vigorously promoted and as (after the 1970 Act) it became clearer that there was a single local authority door upon which to knock, so it became increasingly evident that the sheer volume of referrals made it essential for there to be some discrimination. It was impossible for every referral to be fully investigated and the more of them that were, the more other activities would have to be curtailed. As Jean Packman has noted, 350,000 children were referred to children's departments in England in 1970, of whom 42,000 (12 per cent) were admitted to care and 220,000 (63 per cent) helped in their own homes.[35] Since then comparable national statistics have not been collected but there is little doubt that the number of referrals of children and their families to social services departments has enlarged considerably, especially with heightened public concern about the abuse of children. Referrals calling for some form of exploratory or preventive intervention now threaten to overwhelm the social services. The potential development of prevention has had to be limited because the demand has outstripped the resources available. Even so, we now have situations in both social service departments and in the voluntary societies in which there are many more children and families being supervised or assisted at home than there are children in care – a quite remarkable difference to the long period of severance that we described in earlier chapters.

Factors encouraging the policies and practices of prevention

It is still necessary to explain why this transformation occurred despite these retarding factors. At least three of the reasons have already been discussed in relation to the development of policies for restoration:

- the growing recognition of the damage done to children by separation
- alarm at the escalation in the number of children in care in the 1970s
- the belief that prevention (like restoration) would help to reduce expenditure.

In addition to these influences, however, several others need to be taken into account. One is the existence of the new and professionally-orientated staff who were recruited to the children's departments from 1948 onwards, together with the strengthening of that orientation in social work more generally during the 1970s and '80s. To all intents and purposes a new profession had been created by the 1948 Children Act, and a profession composed of people who were neither steeped in public assistance practices and philosophy nor weighed down by the legacy of the child-savers that pervaded the voluntary sector. It was largely through the leaders in this new profession that the claims of prevention were articulated and acted upon. They saw at first hand the limitations of the care system and became increasingly convinced that, if at all possible, a child should remain at home even though the home might not be providing ideal care. That philosophy was exemplified much later in a report published by the Central Council for Education and Training Social Work entitled *Good Enough Parenting*.[36]

Prevention did not imply a wholesale repudiation of the need to take some children into care. What it maintained, however, was that some parents whose children were candidates for admission to care could be helped to avoid that happening. Of course, it would be foolish to suggest that the new profession of child care carried forward the banner of prevention everywhere and on all occasions. Far from it. During periods of intense upheaval or great pressure, there was always a tendency to retreat to the simplicity and safety of traditional care solutions.[37] Nevertheless, the influence of a prevailing professional ideology favourable to prevention was of great importance in furthering its cause.

That cause was taken up more slowly in the voluntary children's societies, mainly because of the organisational and structural legacies of the child-saving era that were undisturbed by changes comparable with those that occurred in the public sector. For example, the major review of its activities that Barnardo's conducted in 1968 showed that comparatively little work of a preventive nature was being undertaken, not least because there were 'neither the staff, nor the facilities to help problem families *in situ*'.[38] However, as all the main societies have run down their care services in the 1970s and '80s so they have shifted their resources, frequently in imaginative ways, to many kinds of community services to assist families and their children.

In explaining the growth of preventive practices and policies it is also important to recognise the extent to which the ideology fed on itself. The social work world, despite its size, became somewhat akin to a village community where information, rumour and ideas spread quickly. The flow of this communication was facilitated by a number of developments, many of which gained momentum after the Seebohm reforms of the 1970s. A National Bureau for Co-operation in Child Care (now the National Children's Bureau) was created in 1963. There was also the establishment of the British Association of Social Workers with its journals, memoranda, conferences and seminars. Other popular social work and social service magazines became available and widely read. Alongside this, the Central Council for Education and Training Council for Social Work assumed a wider role than the former Central Training Council in Child Care, publishing discussion documents, convening working parties and so on. Pressure groups concerned with children and child care grew rapidly in the 1960s and 1970s, producing their own journals and pamphlets. Child care research expanded and the dissemination of its results to practitioners and managers began to be taken seriously. Whereas, in the 1950s, much of this work of disseminating information and ideas about child care (and 'best practice') had to be done by the inspectors of the Home Office children's department, there is today an extensive communication network that not only brings new issues to the fore but which also imparts extra momentum to those, like the idea of 'prevention', that gain a special foothold.

There is one other factor that has operated to encourage the practice of prevention. Social workers and their managers are always seeking criteria against which performance can be assessed. At one time, as we have seen, it was important to count the number of children rescued or saved – the more the better. Later, in the 1950s, the yardstick of performance was the proportion of children in care who were placed in foster homes. As the rate of foster home failure came to be recognised, this criterion became less compelling. The number of children who could be kept out of care emerged as an alternative indicator of good performance. The work of areas or departments whose 'in care' rates were too far above the norm caused questions to be asked.

A note of caution

In professions and services like social work where it is difficult to assess performance, criteria that offer a firm and quantifiable index tend to be applied with a certain degree of relief, for they provide an anchorage in a turbulent and confusing sea of vacillating expectations and uncertain outcomes. Inasmuch as prevention has been equated with keeping children out of care it has served that purpose, although in the process, the concept of care itself as 'prevention' has lost ground. The stigma of care may well have been sustained by the elevation of the goal of prevention – the need for care was not only the sign of family failure, but of social work failure as well. Within that climate, such strenuous efforts have sometimes been made to keep children out of care that the point at which it was necessary in their best interests has passed, unnoticed.

III Permanency planning

Maluccio and his colleagues have argued that 'permanency planning encompasses both prevention and rehabilitation'.[39] Certainly, that is how it has now come to be viewed. The basic assumption is that children must have stable homes, reliable relationships and committed care if they are to enjoy the security that every child needs and is entitled to expect. These principles came to be expressed in terms of the 'rights' of a child to a permanent home. However, if this were to be attained for the child in care, deliberate steps had to be taken: hence permanency planning.

Clearly permanence could be achieved (as far as permanence is ever possible) if the child's parents could be helped to provide it, either by 'preventive' aid or by being assisted to have back a child who had been in care. However, the roots of the idea of 'permanency planning' were more firmly located in the field of adoption.

Adoption

The 1975 Children Act provides a convenient point from which to trace the history of the idea. The Act contained a number of measures that made it easier for children to be adopted without the approval of their birth parents and for them to be 'released for adoption' without a specific application for an order having been made. Adoption agencies could then seek adoptive parents secure in the knowledge that permission had already been obtained. The legislation also enabled local authorities to pay allowances to facilitate the adoption of children in care. Furthermore, provision was made for courts, under certain circumstances, to make custodianship orders that invested foster parents and relatives with clear rights once they had been looking after a child for a specified period. Although custodianship did not extinguish parental rights entirely (and, in any case, the orders expired when the child reached 18) it did limit the power of birth parents to recover the child or to intervene.

It was some time before all the sections of the 1975 Act were implemented and some provisions, such as custodianship, have been little used. However, it was a landmark because it reflected the gathering of new forces and exposed more clearly than before deep-seated conflicts in child care policy. In part, the Act followed from the recommendations of the Houghton Committee on adoption[40] but that, in its turn, was set up in response to a coalition of pressures. In particular, there was a growing concern about children in care who were neither being returned to their parents, nor being found an alternative permanent home. That concern was intensified as a result of the publication in 1973 of Jane Rowe's book *Children Who Wait*. Likewise, it was already plain from a number of studies that long-term foster care was far from universally successful.[41] Not only did children in care 'wait' but, whilst waiting, many of them suffered the damaging upheavals of several different placements. Neither foster care nor residential care appeared to be able to ensure a lasting alternative for children who did not return to their parents.

Research findings played a vital part in challenging some of the rather comfortable and reassuring notions that had prevailed about the benign nature of 'care', especially public care after the reforms of 1948. In this there are obvious parallels with the role played by research in the 'rediscovery of poverty' that occurred at roughly the same time.[42]

American influences on British adoption and permanency policies

A second influence on the reassessment of care policies for separated children came from the United States. Of course, child care, as other areas of social policy, had been affected by ideas from overseas before. One is hardly likely to find a history of the subject that does not mention, for example, the impact made upon the British reformatory school movement by the system adopted at Mettrai in France,[43] and there is little doubt that the early child emigrationists of the 19th century were inspired by the work of the American Charles Loring Brace, who arranged for thousands of children from the slums of New York and elsewhere to be sent to farms in the new west.[44] Likewise, Florence Davenport Hill's championship of boarding-out in the 1860s derived from the information that she collected about the use of the system in Australia.[45] Even so, such foreign influences were erratic and their effect uncertain. Much depended upon the skill and energy with which they were taken up by groups in this country. That was certainly true of the wave of new ideas and examples which arrived from America in the 1970s indicating both the desirability and feasibility of 'permanency planning'.

These ideas were perhaps best captured by Goldstein, Freud and Solnit in their book, *Beyond the Best Interests of the Child*, published in 1973[46] Thoburn has summarised the message that these authors delivered in the following way:

> '[they] argued that those responsible for choosing the "least detrimental alternative" placements for children in care should acknowledge that the prime need of these children was to live with parent figures with whom they could be sure they would remain. If birth parents were unable to offer this security, then their place should be taken, within time limits appropriate to each child's age, by "psychological parents", either foster parents with whom they were already living, or new parents willing and able to take on this role.'[47]

Furthermore, the American authors argued that, where this was necessary, contact with the birth parents was detrimental to the establishment of the new attachments upon which the success of the placement depended. Since, ultimately, it was only possible to terminate such contact by the legal extinction of the birth parents' rights, the conclusion to be drawn was that only through adoption could the necessary severance be achieved.

The force of that conclusion was strengthened by the growing evidence from the United States that many more children could be satisfactorily adopted than it had been commonly believed: handicapped children, black children and older children. Pioneering programmes to do just that were described and reported, the best known probably being Spaulding for Children in Michigan – a scheme that had arisen from the work of a parents' group, the Council on Adoptable Children. There are fascinating questions about the reasons why such developments emerged and were so energetically pursued in the United States in the late 1960s and early 1970s. We cannot go into them here, except perhaps to suggest that the child-saving ideology survived longer in that country because of the prominence of voluntary, rather than public, child care agencies and because of the continuing strength of the evangelical influence. Certainly, the laws of some states provided a much greater opportunity than in Britain for the consent of birth parents to adoption to be dispensed with.

The establishment of the permanency movement in Britain

Whatever the reasons for its development in the United States, the 'permanency movement' became established in this country in the latter years of the 1970. Its emergence as a principal theme in current child care owes a great deal to the enthusiasm with which the cause was taken up by an assortment of adoption groups in the voluntary sector. Established organisations set up new schemes (such as Barnardo's New Families Project) and independent initiatives were inaugurated (such as the Adoption Resource Exchange and the Parent to Parent Information on Adoption Service) in order to bring together adopters and children available for adoption. In the 1980s British Agencies for Adoption and Fostering launched Be My Parent, a scheme based upon the distribution of photographs of children who had proved difficult to place. More local authorities began to advertise in newspapers and elsewhere for long-term foster parents to care for particular children. Indeed, the permanency movement expanded to incorporate long-term foster care and, in doing so, enlisted the support of groups such as the National Foster Care Association that represents foster parents.

Thus, the momentum gained by the permanency movement was, at least in the first place, attributable to the energies of a relatively small group whose primary interest was in the adoption of children. Thoburn refers to it as 'a small band of converts', adding that 'no-one who had contact with workers in this field in the late '70s could fail to notice the elements of faith and mission in their work'.[48] Perhaps for this reason the ideas spread, but in spreading they were modified and reinterpreted.

By the 1980s the recognition of the need to plan for the futures of children in care had permeated many social services departments and although that entailed the reconsideration of the possibilities of adoption for some, it also prompted closer attention to restoration and, by extension, to prevention. It emphasised, too, the need for the regular and systematic review of each child in care, in order to check what had been done and what required to be done. The dangers of drift and indecision were recognised, if not always avoided. Perhaps, in that sense, the most important long-term impact of 'permanency planning' will be on 'planning'. If that is done well, the goal of stable long-term care for children is more likely to be achieved.

Opposition to the permanency movement

However, it should not be assumed that the quest for permanence, at least inasmuch as it entailed permanent separation from parents, met with no opposition. Indeed, it was inevitable that it would, for it raised in stark relief the conflict of interests and rights that child care has embodied from its earliest beginnings. It is not simply a matter of the competing rights of birth parents, foster parents or children. There is also the potential tension between the right of the child to be with, know and feel identified with the family of its birth, and the equally important right of the child to enjoy a secure, stable, untroubled and loving home. In the majority of families these rights exist in harmony most of the time; once separations occur, however (whether they be through divorce or admission to care) a conflict between them is exposed that is not easily resolved, especially where it is unclear, because of uncertainties about the future, where the best interests of the child (both short-term and long-term) lie.

Opposition to the general orientation of the permanency movement came from a number of quarters. There were those, for example, who although not denying the need to secure permanent alternative families for some children, considered that too little was done (and often too late) to enable birth parents to fulfil their duties, and thus exercise their rights, with respect to their children. A rush to permanence both denied that possibility and reinforced the roles of 'incompetent' or 'uncaring' parent in which structural forces had cast unfortunate people.[49] What was wanted, it was claimed, was not more adoption but a vastly enlarged investment in preventive services and preventive environments of all kinds.

A second shaft of opposition to the underlying rationale of permanence came from black people. Permanence for black or mixed race children had been achieved almost wholly (until recently) by placing them with white adopters or white foster parents.[50] The thrust of the black opposition was not that children did not need a permanent home, but that not enough had been done to make sure that that home was a black home. Indeed, it was maintained that the placement of a black child in a white family was blatantly *against* his or her best interests, since a clear sense of racial identity was crucial in a racist society.[51] Again, the criticism directed at the permanence movement was not that it sought permanent solutions for the care of children but of the form that these were taking, of the negative images of black parents that it created (and depended upon) and, last but not least, that the problems it strove to overcome could have been avoided in many cases had parents in distress been given more help – and had they not had to live in such a hostile and discriminating society.

A further source of opposition to the permanency movement was to be found amongst parents of children in care and in the (rather few) groups that represented their views. Inasmuch as policies of permanence were seen as a shift towards severance, such parents felt threatened – it might happen to them. Those fears were, of course, heightened by the difficulties that some of them encountered in obtaining access to their children.[52] Having your child admitted or committed to care seemed to be a more hazardous business as the cause of 'permanence' gained wider currency.

Partly as a result of these counter-currents the idea of permanency planning has undergone refinements and adaptations. Consequently, its influence on child care policy and practice has become more general, and ceased to be associated primarily with adoption. Nevertheless, in whatever their particular forms, permanency planning, prevention and restoration have brought conflicts and contradictions to the surface which had gone largely unacknowledged before. Though often painful, the need to confront the claims of contending rights and interests, especially those of each individual child, may well be the most powerful force for beneficial change in the history of child care.

IV A final comment

Today's problems, policies and controversies cannot be understood without reference to their historical backgrounds. The slate is rarely, if ever, wiped clean. Inasmuch as the care of separated children, or of children at risk, is set within legal, financial and organisational frameworks, it is subject to the continuities and constraints that they embody as well as to the interests which they reflect, create and sustain. Ideas may *seem* to be new but a little exploration in the past will often reveal their antecedents, different in detail perhaps, but surprisingly similar in their essential characteristics. The current social ills which give rise to the need for child care services seem to bear little resemblance to those of the past, yet can be found to display remarkable likenesses once more is understood about their root causes. However far-reaching changes may appear to be, their origins lie in what has gone before. The present is constructed from the past.

Notes

1 Introduction

1 Three well-known examples are Lucy Sinclair, *Bridgeburn Days*, Gollancz, 1956; Janet Hitchman, *King of the Barbareens*, Putnam, 1960, and T. O'Neill, *A Place Called Hope*, Blackwell, 1981.

2 See, for example, P. Thompson, *The Voice of the Past*, OUP, 1978.

3 For an account of these procedures and the criticisms of the methods see G. Wagner, *Barnardo*, Weidenfeld and Nicholson, 1979, and J. Rose, *For the Sake of the Children*, Hodder and Stoughton, 1987.

4 For a moving example of how, looking back, lives are evaluated see A. B. Facey, *A Fortunate Life*, Penguin Books, Australia, 1981.

5 *Report of the Departmental Committee to Inquire into the Existing Systems of Maintenance and Education of Children under the Charge of Managers of District Schools and Boards of Guardians in the Metropolis*, vol I 'Report', c 8027, and vol II 'Evidence', c 8032, HMSO, 1896.

6 Registration was introduced by the Children and Young Persons Act, 1933.

7 See R. A. Parker, 'The Gestation of Reform: the 1948 Children Act' in P. Bean and S. MacPherson (eds), *Approaches to Welfare*, Routledge and Kegan Paul, 1983.

8 See S. M. Ferguson and H. Fitzgerald, *Studies in the Social Services* (History of the Second World War Series), HMSO and Longmans, 1954, p 233.

9 B. R. Mitchell and P. Deane, *Abstract of British Historical Statistical Sources*, Cambridge University Press, 1971, pp 19–21.

10 *Ibid*, pp 36–7.

11 For the latter see especially M. Carpenter, *Reformatory Schools for the Children of the Perishing and Dangerous Classes and for Juvenile Offenders*, Gilpin, 1851. (Republished by Woburn Books, 1968.)

12 But see, for a general account of illegitimacy and its treatment, I. Pinchbeck and M. Hewitt, *Children in English Society*, vol II, Routledge and Kegan Paul, 1973, ch, XIX.

13 See *Annual Reports of the Board of Supervision and the Local Government Board for Scotland*.

14 See J. Parr, *Labouring Children: British Apprentices to Canada, 1869-1924*, Croom Helm/McGill – Queen's University Press, 1980.

15 *Report of the Care of Children Committee* (Curtis), cmd 6922, HMSO, 1946, p 10.

16 This was the Poor Law Board until 1871, then the Local Government Board until 1918, and then the Ministry of Health.

17 By the Unemployment Assistance Act, which transferred responsibility for the payment of most unemployment assistance committees to the central Unemployment Assistance from the local public assistance committees to the central Unemployment Assistance Board which became the Assistance Board during the war and was absorbed into the National Assistance Board in 1948.

18 For example, *Report of Inquiry by C. F. G. Masterman, MP, into Charges made concerning the Management of Heswell Nautical School*, cd 5541, HMSO, 1911, and, much later, *Administration of Punishment at Court Lees Approved School, Report of Inquiry by Mr Edward Gibbens, QC*, cmnd 3367, HMSO, 1967.

2 The age of separation

1 For an interesting interpretation see A. M. Platt, *The Child Savers*, University of Chicago Press, 1969.

2 Canon Bennett, *Father Nugent of Liverpool*, Liverpool Catholic Children's Protection Society, 1949.

3 Barnardo, *Something Attempted, Something Done!* Shaw, 1889, p 15.

4 Figures derived from the annual publication, *Catholic Directory*, Universe Publications.

5 *Annual Report of the Waifs and Strays Society*, 1898, p 17.

6 *Annual Report of the Ministry of Health, 1919–20*, cmd 933 (part 2), HMSO, 1920, and for 1933–4, cmd 4664, p 241. It should be noted that each year some Homes closed or had their certificates withdrawn, whilst new ones were brought on to the list.

7 *Report of the Care of Children Committee* (Curtis), *op cit*, table 1, p 12.

8 See, for example, Home Office, *Third Report on the Work of the Children's Branch*, HMSO, 1925, p 34.

9 See R. A. Parker, 'The Historical Background' in I. Sinclair (ed), *Residential Care: the Research Reviewed*, vol 2 of the Wagner Report, HMSO, 1988, pp 29–30.

10 Barnardo's, *Annual Report for 1890*, 1891.

11 Barnardo's, *Annual Report for 1901*, 1902.

12 *Annual Report of the Waifs and Strays Society for 1904*, 1905.

13 For a detailed account of these developments and others associated with the protection of children, see, G. K. Behlmer, *Child Abuse and Moral Reform in England, 1870-1908,* Stanford University Press, 1982.

14 I. Pinchbeck and M. Hewitt, *Children in English Society,* vol II, *op cit,* p 382.

15 Guardianship of Infants Act, 1925. It should be noted, however, that unmarried mothers had always had rights over their children, although their circumstances were usually such that they were of little assistance to them in the arrangement of their care in adversity.

16 My unpublished research on two series of Home Office letterbooks. After 1894 whenever it was proposed to emigrate a child who had been committed to a fit person, the approval of the Secretary of State had to be obtained. There are 'approval letters' on file, there-fore, and, with patience, they can be counted. See PRO, HO 152, vols 1-14: 'Miscellaneous Domestic Correspondence'. After June 1905 the letters are contained in HO 167; the 'Child Entry Books'.

17 Barnardo, *op cit,* p 181.

18 Home Office, *Third Report on the work of the Children's Branch,* HMSO, p 35.

19 See J. Parr, *op cit,* for an account of the emigration of Barnardo children and also G. Wagner, *Children of the Empire,* Weidenfeld and Nicholson, 1982.

20 G. Wagner, *Barnardo, op cit,* p 218.

21 *Ibid,* p 219.

22 *Ibid,* p 235.

23 *Hansard's Parliamentary Debates* (HL), vol 353, June 5, 1891, col 1696.

24 *Hansard* (HL), *op cit.*

25 See Behlmer, *op cit,* for a fuller coverage of the issue.

26 Home Office, *Sixth Report on the Work of the Children's Department,* HMSO, 1951; calculated from table 2, p 148.

27 The Children Bill, 1989, was based upon the white paper *The Law on Child Care and Family Services* (Department of Health, *et al,* cm 62, HMSO, 1987.

28 See the *Report of the Child Adoption Committee,* cmd 1254, HMSO, 1921.

29 J. Stroud, *Thirteen Penny Stamps: the Story of the Church of England Children's Society, from its beginnings as 'Waifs and Strays',* Hodder and Stoughton, 1971, p 176.

30 Home Office, *Fifth Report on the Work of the Children's Branch,* HMSO, 1938, p 104.

31 J. Rowe and L. Lambert, *Children Who Wait*, Association of British Adoption Agencies, 1973.

32 S. Millham, *et al, Lost in Care: Problems of Maintaining Links between Children in Care and their Families*, Gower, 1986.

3 Reformatory and industrial schools – an institutional solution

1   J. Carlebach, *Caring for Children in Trouble*, Routledge and Kegan Paul, 1970. See Chapter 1 for an account of the founding of the Royal Philanthropic School in 1788.

2   A good and informative example is an anonymous article entitled 'Schools of Industry' in *Chambers' Miscellany*, 1844, but see also the *Report of the Select Committee on Criminal and Destitute Juveniles*, 1852.

3   See G. Stedman Jones, *Outcast London: A Study in the Relationship between Classes in Victorian Society*, Penguin Books, 1976 (first published OUP, 1971), for an excellent account of the impact of these conditions.

4   *Report of the Royal Commission on Reformatory and Industrial Schools*, c 3876 – I, 'Minutes of Evidence', HMSO, 1884, para 22.

5   *The Twenty-Seventh Annual Report of the Inspector of Reformatory and Industrial Schools*, c 4147, 1884, p 21.

6   *Ibid*, para 26. The *Annual Reports of the Inspector of Reformatory and Industrial Schools* provide detailed statistical information.

7   It should be noted that some schools were subsequently established and run by local school boards.

8   *Twenty-Seventh Annual Report of the Inspector, op cit*, calculated from statement of 'Receipts and Expenditure', p 36.

9   *Report of the Royal Commission on Reformatory and Industrial Schools, op cit*, 'Report', paras 13-14, p xv.

10 Home Office, *Report on the Work of the Children's Branch*, HMSO, 1923, p 29.

11 *Ibid*, quoted p 26.

12 G. Rose, *Schools for Young Offenders*, Tavistock, 1967, p 3.

13 *Ibid*, p 4.

14 Barnardo, *op cit*, p 175.

15 *Chambers' Miscellany, op cit*, p 4.

16 *Report of the Departmental Committee on Reformatory and Industrial Schools*, vol 1 'Report and Appendices'. c 8204 and vol 2 'Evidence and Index', c 8290, HMSO, 1896.

17 *Report of the Departmental Committee on Reformatory and Industrial Schools*, cd 8939, HMSO, 1913.

18 Figures obtained from: Home Office, *Report on the Work of the Children's Branch*, HMSO, 1923 and Home Office, *Fifth Report on the Work of the Children's Branch*, HMSO, 1938.

19 *Ibid*.

20 *Ibid*.

21 *Report of Inquiry by C. F. G. Masterman, MP, into Charges made concerning the Management of Heswell Nautical School*, op cit.

22 *Report of the Departmental Committee*, 1913, op cit.

23 Carlebach, *op cit*, p 89.

24 Home Office, *Second Report on the Work of the Children's Branch*, HMSO, 1924, p 23.

25 Home Office, *Reports on the Work of the Children's Branch*, HMSO, 1923 and 1928.

26 Home Office, *Third Report on the Work of the Children's Branch*, HMSO, 1925, p 25.

27 *Ibid*, p 58.

28 *Report of the Departmental Committee on the Treatment of Young Offenders*, cmd 2831, HMSO, 1927.

29 Home Office, *Sixth Report on the Work of the Children's Department*, HMSO, 1951, p 64.

30 Calculated from statistics provided in the 1938 and 1951 *Reports on the Work of the Children's Department*, op cit.

31 Calculated from statistics provided in the 1925 and 1938 *Reports on the Work of the Children's Branch*, op cit.

32 See 1938 *Report on the Work of the Children's Branch*, op cit, table 1, p 131 (note, in 1936 only 3 of the children made subject to fit person orders were offenders; in 1950 there were 824). See also *Sixth Report on the Work of the Children's Department*, op cit, p 10. Figures are for England and Wales.

33 Home Office, *Eighth Report on the Work of the Children's Department*, HMSO, 1961, p 44.

34 Home Office, *Report on the Work of the Children's Department, 1961-63*, HC 155, HMSO, 1964, p 33.

35 J. Packman, *The Child's Generation*, Blackwell and Robertson, 1975, provides a good account of these developments in Chapter 6, as does P. Parsloe, *Juvenile Justice*, Routledge and Kegan Paul, 1978.

36 Labour Party, *Crime – A Challenge to us All* (Longford report), 1964.

37 There was first *The Child, the Family and the Young Offender,* cmnd 2742, HMSO, 1965 and then *Children in Trouble,* cmnd 3601, HMSO, 1968.

38 For example, Home Office, *Disturbances at the Carlton Approved School on 29th and 30th August, 1959, Report of Inquiry by Mr Victor Durand, QC,* cmnd 937, HMSO, 1960, and Home Office, *Administration of Punishment at Court Lees Approved School, op cit.*

4 The boarding-out of poor law children – a mirror on residential care

1   F. Davenport Hill, *Children of the State: the Training of Juvenile Paupers,* Macmillan, 1868.

2   The deputation that met the president, George Goschen, in May, 1870, included: Hannah Archer, Louisa Bourcherett, Frances Power Cobbe, and the sisters Florence and Joanna Davenport (sisters to Octavia Hill).

3   Appendix A to the *Annual Report of the Poor Law Board, 1870-1,* c 396, HMSO, 1871, p iv.

4   *Ibid,* p 15.

5   Regulation No 16, Article V of the *Boarding-Out of Pauper Children,* General Order, No 8, 1870.

6   Appendix B to the *Annual Report of the Local Government Board, 1874-5,* 1875, report No 15, 'Swansea Union – Boarding-Out of Pauper Children', p 172.

7   *Annual Report of the Local Government Board, 1888-9,* c 5813, HMSO, 1889, p xcvi.

8   *Report of the Departmental Committee to Inquire into the Existing Systems of Maintenance and Education of Children . . . in the Metropolis, op cit.*

9   See for example, N. Middleton, *When Family Failed,* Gollancz, 1971, p 225.

10 See *Annual Reports of the Ministry of Health* for the respective years. See also Middleton, *op cit.*

11 *Annual Report of the Ministry of Health, 1931-2,* cmd 4113, HMSO, 1932, p 208.

12 *Annual Report of the Ministry of Health, 1934-5,* cmd 4978, HMSO, 1935, p 228.

13 *Ibid.*

14 See *Report of the Care of Children Committee, op cit,* table III, p 25.

15 *Ibid,* p 152.

16 *Ibid*, p 25.

17 *Ibid*, p 15.

18 *Ibid*, p 153.

19 For a fuller account, see R. M. Titmuss, *Problems of Social Policy*, HMSO, 1950.

20 See the *Report on the Circumstances which led to the Boarding-Out of Dennis and Terence O'Neill at Bank Farm, Minsterley, and the steps taken to supervise their Welfare* (Monckton), cmd 6636, HMSO, 1945.

21 For a fuller account see R. A. Parker, 'The Gestation of Reform', *op cit*.

22 Scottish Home Department, *Report of the Committee on Homeless Children* (Clyde), cmd 6911, HMSO, 1946.

23 Curtis Committee report, *op cit*, appendix 1, 'Training in Child Care', p 184. For an account of the influence of the early location of social work training in universities in Britain, see R. A. Parker, 'Social Ills and Public Remedies', in W. Robson (ed), *Man and the Social Sciences*, LSE/Allen and Unwin, 1972.

24 Home Office, Children's Department, Circular No 160/1948, 'Children Act 1948', 8 July, 1948, para 28.

25 Home Office, Circular No 258/1952, para 2.

26 *Sixth Report on the Work of the Children's Department*, *op cit*, p 18.

27 *Sixth Report from the Select Committee on Estimates, Session 1951-2 (Child Care)*, HC 235, HMSO, para 14, p xiv.

28 'Departmental Reply to the Sixth Report from the Select Committee on Estimates, Session 1951-2 (Child Care)', appendix 1 to the *13th Report of the Select Committee on Estimates 1951-2*, HC 328, HMSO.

29 See *Children in Care in England and Wales, 1952*, cmd 8910, HMSO, 1953.

30 Home Office, *Seventh Report on the Work of the Children's Department*, HMSO, 1955, p 28.

31 P. G. Gray and E. A. Parr, *Children in Care and the Recruitment of Foster Parents*, Social Survey, SS 249, 1957.

32 R. Holman, 'The Place of Fostering in Social Work', *British Journal of Social Work*, vol 5, No 1, 1975.

33 Home Office, *The Boarding-Out of Children Regulations*, 1955, SI 1377.

34 G. B. Trasler, *In Place of Parents*, Routledge and Kegan Paul, 1960.

35 R. A. Parker, *Decision in Child Care: A Study of Prediction in Fostering*, Allen and Unwin, 1966.

36 V. George, *Foster Care*, Routledge and Kegan Paul, 1970.

37 *Seventh Report on the Work of the Children's Department*, *op cit*, pp 8-9.

38 DHSS, *Report of the Committee of Inquiry into the Care and Supervision Provided in Relation to Maria Colwell*, HMSO, 1974.

39 See, for example, Department of the Environment, District Audit, *The Provision of Child Care: A Study of Eight Local Authorities in England and Wales – Final Report*, HMSO, 1981.

40 Department of Health, *Children in Care of Local Authorities at 31st March 1986 – England*, A/F 86/12, Government Statistical Service, 1988 and Welsh Office, *Children in Care or Under Supervision Orders in Wales, Year ended 31.3.86*, Government Statistical Service, 1987.

41 For a fuller discussion of the inter-connections between foster-care and residential care see R. A. Parker, 'Residential Care for Children' in I. Sinclair (ed), *Residential Care: the Research Reviewed, op cit*.

5 Comparisons and contrasts

1   Barnardo's, *Annual Report for 1894*, p 66.

2   J. Rose, *op cit*, p 118.

3   T. J. Barnardo, *The Rescue of Waifs*, Barnardo's Homes, nd, p 13.

4   J. Rose, *op cit*, p 112.

5   See, for example, Fowler to Barnardo, 25th July, 1905, Liverpool University Archive, d 239, c 1/1, pp 65-6.

6   J. Rose, *op cit*, esp ch 7.

7   Calculated from annual statistics of *Children in the Care of Local Authorities in England and Wales* (Home Office, then DHSS, now DH).

8   Part of a vigorous correspondence in *The Times*, 6th, 7th, 9th and 10th November, 1874.

9   *Annual Report of the Local Government Board for 1873-4*, c 1071, HMSO, 1874, appendix, report No 22, Mrs Nassau Senior, 'Education of Girls in Pauper Schools'.

10 Unpublished research, private communication.

11 *Report of the Departmental Committee to Inquire into the Existing Systems of Maintenance and Education of Children . . . in the Metropolis*, vol II 'Evidence', *op cit*, p 502.

12 Again, I am indebted to Harriet Ward for alerting me to this aspect of the history.

13 NCH, *Annual Report for 1907-8*, p 15.

14 A. A. Jacka, *The Story of the Children's Home, 1869-1969*, NCH, 1969, p 33.

15 NCH, *Annual Report for 1899-1900*, p 13.

16   NCH, *Annual Report for 1907-8*, p 15.
17   NCH, *Annual Report for 1912-13*, p 25.
18   NCH, *Annual Report for 1919-20*, statistical tables.
19   *Catholic Directory, op cit.*
20   N. Waugh (ed), *These, My Little Ones: the Origins, Purposes and Development of the Incorporated Society of the Crusade of Rescue and Homes for Destitute Catholic Children*, Sands, 1911, p 155.
21   *Ibid*, p 156.

6 Modern themes

1   *Report of the Care of Children Committee, op cit*, p 60.
2   *Ibid*, p 83.
3   Scottish Home Department, *Report of the Committee on Homeless Children, op cit*, pp 29-30.
4   Children Act, 1948, section 1(3) a and b.
5   *Parliamentary Debates* (Lords), session 1947-8, vol 153, 2R Children Bill, col 937.
6   Home Office, *Seventh Report on the Work of the Children's Department*, HMSO, 1955, p 3.
7   See, R. A. Parker, 'The Gestation of Reform', *op cit.*
8   This body of evidence was synthesised by John Bowlby in the 1940s and later published as *Maternal Care and Mental Health*, WHO, monograph series, No 2, 1951. Its influence on child care, especially through the training courses, was considerable.
9   Home Office, *Eighth Report on the Work of the Children's Department*, HMSO, 1961, p 17.
10   See, for example, appendix 1 'Training in Child Care' in the *Report of the Care of Children Committee, op cit*, pp 184-6.
11   Home Office, *Children in Care in England and Wales, March, 1963*, cmnd 2240, HMSO, 1963, table 1.
12   Calculated from figures in, Home Office, *Seventh Report, op cit*, tables 2 and 4, pp 153-4.
13   See, E. Farmer and R. A. Parker, *Trials and Tribulations: A Study of Children Placed Home on Trial* (forthcoming).
14   See evidence discussed in R. A. Parker in I. Sinclair (ed), *op cit.*
15   Rowe and Lambert, *op cit.*
16   On this general theme, see R. A. Parker, *Planning for Deprived Children*, NCH, 1971.
17   See Millham, *et al, op cit*, ch 1.

18   These and other figures in this section have been calculated from
     the annual statistics on *Children in the Care of Local Authorities in
     England and Wales, op cit.*

19   Much of the increase in the number of care orders being made in
     the 1970s was accounted for by more young offenders being
     committed to care instead of being made subject to the former
     approved school orders; but it was also a reflection of a fall in the
     admission of voluntary cases, to some extent because of the
     emergence of better preventive policies for this category. The
     marked reduction in the number and proportion of delinquents being
     committed to care did not occur until the 1980s, partly as a result
     of diversionary policies like intermediate treatment, but also, because
     of the weakening of the 1969 philosophy that juvenile offending
     should be treated as a welfare matter, more youngsters began to
     be found in the penal system. See, G. Stewart and N. Tutt, *Children
     in Custody*, Avebury, 1987.

20   See, R. A. Parker, 'Child Care: the Roots of a Dilemma', *Political
     Quarterly*, vol 57, No 3, July–September, 1986.

21   *A Child in Trust: the Report of the Panel of Inquiry into the Circumstances
     Surrounding the Death of Jasmine Beckford*, London Borough of Brent,
     1985.

22   *Report of the Inquiry into Child Abuse in Cleveland, 1987*, cm 412,
     HMSO, 1988.

23   Children Act, 1975, sect 56. The section applied equally to children
     in the care of local authorities and voluntary organisations. The
     authorities could waive the requirement if they saw fit to do so.

24   *Ibid.* Section 14 1(b), for example, provided that, under certain
     circumstances, the agreement of the natural parents to adoption
     could be dispensed with.

25   Criminal Justice Act, 1982, sect 22.

26   Sometimes young offenders were not removed from home when a
     care order was made because there were no vacancies in an appro-
     priate establishment. But sometimes, at least so magistrates tended
     to believe, it was because social workers did not share the court's
     view about the necessity for removal.

28   See, Packman, *op cit*, ch 4, for an account of some of these and
     later developments.

29   Home Office, *Report of the Committee on Children and Young Persons*
     (Ingleby), cmnd 1191, HMSO, 1960.

30 For a discussion of the difficulties inherent in the provision of 'corporate care' see R. A. Parker (ed), *Caring for Separated Children*, Macmillan, 1980. ch 5.

31 See, R. A. Parker, 'Collaboration in Child Care', in M. L. Kellmer Pringle (ed), *Caring for Children*, Longmans, 1969.

32 Joint Circular from the Home Office (157/50), the Ministry of Health (78/50) and Ministry of Education (225/50), on *Children Neglected or Ill-Treated in their Own Homes*, 1950.

33 Children and Young Persons Act, 1963, sect 1(1).

34 Home Office, Department of Education and Science, Ministry of Health and the Ministry of Housing and Local Government, *Report of the Committee on Local Authority and Allied Personal Social Services* (Seebohm), cmnd 3703, 1968. See especially the chapter on 'Prevention'.

35 Packman, *op cit*, p 69.

36 Central Council for Education and Training in Social Work, *Good Enough Parenting*, 1978.

37 John Stroud captures such a time of upheaval in his novel *The Shorn Lamb* (Longmans, 1962), set in the early years after the establishment of children's departments.

38 Barnardo's, *A Review of the Child Care and Special Education Services in the United Kingdom and Republic of Ireland*, 1968.

39 A. N. Maluccio, E. Fein and K. A. Olmstead, *Permanency Planning for Children: Concepts and Methods*, Tavistock, 1986.

40 *Report of the Departmental Committee on the Adoption of Children* (Houghton), cmnd 5107, HMSO, 1972.

41 See, for example, Parker, *Decision in Child Care*, Trasler and George, *op cit*.

42 For example, P. Townsend and D. Wedderburn, *The Poor and the Poorest*, Bell, 1965. The growth of social research in the 1960s is a fascinating phenomenon in its own right. It was not unrelated to the expansion of universities, to the establishment of the Social Science Research Council and to the greater involvement of central government departments in developing their own research capacity (for example, the Home Office Research Unit) and in commissioning studies from outside bodies.

43 For example, Pinchbeck and Hewitt, *op cit*, pp 468 and 474.

44 E. Brace (ed), *The Life of Charles Loring Brace*, Scribners (New York), 1894, esp ch 6.

45 F. Davenport Hill, *op cit*.

46 J. Goldstein, A. Freud and A. Solnit, *Beyond the Best Interests of the Child*, Free Press, 1973.

47 J. Thoburn, A. Murdoch and A. O'Brien, *Permanence in Child Care*, Blackwell, 1986.

48 *Ibid*, p 11.

49 For example, B. Jordan, 'Prevention', *Adoption and Fostering*, vol 5, No 3, 1981.

50 See for example, L. Raynor, *Adoption of Non-White Children*, Allen and Unwin, 1970; O. Gill and B. Jackson, *Adoption and Race: Black, Asian and Mixed-Race Children in White Families*, Batsford, 1983.

51 J. Small, 'Transracial Placements: Conflicts and Contradictions' in S. Ahmed, J. Cheetham and J. Small (eds), *Social Work with Black Children and their Families*, Batsford, 1985.

52 S. Millham, *et al*, *Access Disputes in Child Care*, Gower, 1989.

Bibliography

Books and Articles

AHMED, S., CHEETHAM, J., AND SMALL, J. (eds), *Social Work with Black Children and their Families*, Batsford, 1985.

ANON, 'Schools of Industry', *Chambers' Miscellany*, Chambers, 1844.

BARNARDO, T. J., *Something Attempted, Something Done!*, Shaw, 1889. *The Rescue of Waifs*, Barnardo's Homes, nd.

BARNARDO'S, *A Review of the Child Care and Special Education Services in the United Kingdom and Republic of Ireland*, 1968.

BEAN, P., AND MACPHERSON, S. (eds), *Approaches to Welfare*, Routledge and Kegan Paul, 1983.

BEHLMER, G. K., *Child Abuse and Moral Reform in England, 1870-1908*, Stanford University Press, 1982.

BENNETT, CANON, *Father Nugent of Liverpool*, Liverpool Catholic Children's Protection Society, 1949.

BOWLBY, J., *Maternal Care and Mental Health*, WHO, Monograph Series, No 2, 1951.

BRACE, E. (ed), *The Life of Charles Loring Brace*, Scribners (New York), 1894.

CARLEBACH, J., *Caring for Children in Trouble*, Routledge and Kegan Paul, 1970.

CARPENTER, M., *Reformatory Schools for the Children of the Perishing and Dangerous Classes and for Juvenile Offenders*, Gilpin, 1851 (republished by Woburn Books, 1968).

CENTRAL COUNCIL FOR EDUCATION AND TRAINING IN SOCIAL WORK, *Good Enough Parenting*, 1978.

FACEY, A. B., *A Fortunate Life*, Penguin Books, Australia, 1981.

FARMER, E., AND PARKER, R. A., *Trials and Tribulations: A Study of Children Placed Home on Trial* (forthcoming).

FERGUSON, S. M., AND FITZGERALD, H., *Studies in the Social Services* (History of the Second World War Series), HMSO and Longmans, 1954.

GEORGE, V., *Foster Care*, Routledge and Kegan Paul, 1970.

GILL, O., AND JACKSON, B., *Adoption and Race: Black, Asian and Mixed-Race Children in White Families*, Batsford, 1983.

GOLDSTEIN, J., FREUD, A., AND SOLNIT, A., *Beyond the Best Interests of the Child*, Free Press, 1973.

GRAY, P. G. AND PARR, E. A., *Children in Care and the Recruitment of Foster Parents*, Social Survey, SS 249, 1957.

HILL, F. DAVENPORT, *Children of the State: the Training of Juvenile Paupers*, Macmillan, 1868.

HITCHMAN, J., *King of the Barbareens*, Putnam, 1960.

HOLMAN, R., 'The Place of Fostering in Social Work', *British Journal of Social Work*, vol 5, No 1, 1975.

JACKA, A. A., *The Story of the Children's Home, 1869-1969*, NCH, 1969.

JONES, G. STEADMAN, *Outcast London: A Study in the Relationship between Classes in Victorian Society*, Penguin Books, 1976 (first published OUP, 1971).

JORDAN, B., 'Prevention', *Adoption and Fostering*, vol 5, No 3, 1981.

LABOUR PARTY, *Crime – A Challenge to us All* (Longford Report), 1964.

MALUCCIO, A. N., FEIN, E., AND OLMSTEAD, K. A., *Permanency Planning for Children: Concepts and Methods*, Tavistock, 1986.

MIDDLETON, N., *When Family Failed*, Gollancz, 1971.

MILLHAM, S., *et al, Lost in Care: Problems of Maintaining Links between Children in Care and their Families*, Gower, 1986.
Access Disputes in Child Care, Gower, 1989.

MITCHELL, B. R., AND DEANE, P., *Abstract of British Historical Statistical Sources*, Cambridge University Press, 1971.

O'NEILL, T., *A Place Called Hope*, Blackwell, 1981.

PACKMAN, J., *The Child's Generation*, Blackwell and Robertson, 1975.

PARKER, R. A., *Decision in Child Care: A Study of Prediction in Fostering*, Allen and Unwin, 1966.
Planning for Deprived Children, NCH, 1971.
'Child Care: the Roots of a Dilemma', *Political Quarterly*, vol 57, No 3, July–September, 1986.

PARKER, R. A., (ed), *Caring for Separated Children*, Macmillan, 1980.

PARR, J., *Labouring Children: British apprentices to Canada, 1869–1924*, Croom Helm/McGill – Queen's University Press, 1980.

PARSLOE, P., *Juvenile Justice*, Routledge and Kegan Paul, 1978.

PLATT, A. M., *The Child Savers*, University of Chicago Press, 1969.

PINCHBECK, I., AND HEWITT, M., *Children in English Society*, Routledge and Kegan Paul, 1973.

PRINGLE, M. KELLMER, *Caring for Children*, Longmans, 1969.

RAYNOR, L., *Adoption of Non-White Children*, Allen and Unwin, 1970.

ROBSON, W. (ed), *Man and the Social Sciences*, LSE/Allen and Unwin, 1972.

ROSE, G., *Schools for Young Offenders*, Tavistock, 1967.

ROSE. J., *For the Sake of the Children*, Hodder and Stoughton, 1987.

ROWE, J., AND LAMBERT, L., *Children Who Wait*, Association of British Adoption Agencies, 1973.

SINCLAIR, I. (ed), *Residential Care: The Research Reviewed*, vol 2 of the Wagner Report, HMSO, 1988.

SINCLAIR, L., *Bridgeburn Days*, Gollancz, 1956.

STEWART, G., AND TUTT, N., *Children in Custody*, Avebury, 1987.

STROUD, J., *Thirteen Penny Stamps: the Story of the Church of England Children's Society, from its beginning as 'Waifs and Strays'*, Hodder and Stoughton, 1971.

THOBURN, J., MURDOCH, A., AND O'BRIEN, A., *Permanence in Child Care*, Blackwell, 1986.

THOMPSON, P., *The Voice of the Past*, OUP, 1978.

TITMUSS, R. M., *Problems of Social Policy*, HMSO, 1950.

TOWNSEND, P., AND WEDDERBURN, D., *The Poor and the Poorest*, Bell, 1965.

TRASLER, G. B., *In Place of Parents*, Routledge and Kegan Paul, 1960.

WAGNER, G., *Barnardo*, Weidenfeld and Nicholson, 1979.
Children of the Empire, Weidenfeld and Nicholson, 1982.

WAUGH, N., (ed), *These My Little Ones: the Origins, Purposes and Development of the Incorporated Society of the Crusade of Rescue and Homes for Destitute Catholic Children*, Sands, 1911.

White Papers, Circulars, Statutory Instruments, etc (in chronological order)

Regulation No 16, Article V, general order No 8, *The Boarding-Out of Pauper Children*, 1870.

Home Office Children's Department, circular No 160/1948, *The Children Act 1948*, 1948.

Home Office Children's Department, circular No 258/1952, *The Children Act 1948*, 1952.

Home Office, *The Boarding-Out of Children Regulations*, SI 1377, 1955.

The Child, the Family and the Young Offender, cmnd, 2742, HMSO, 1965.

Children in Trouble, cmnd 3601, HMSO, 1968.

The Law on Child Care and Family Services, cm 62, HMSO, 1987.

Reports of Commissions and Inquiries (in chronological order)

Report of the Royal Commission on Reformatory and Industrial Schools, 'Report', c 3876, 'Minutes of Evidence', c 3876 – I, HMSO, 1884.

Report of the Departmental Committee to Inquire into the Existing Systems of Maintenance and Education of Children under the Charge of the Managers of District Schools and Boards of Guardians in the Metropolis, vol I, 'Report', c 8027, vol II, 'Evidence', c 8032, HMSO, 1896.

Report of the Departmental Committee on Reformatory and Industrial Schools, vol 1, 'Report and Appendices', c 8204, vol 2, 'Evidence and Index', c 8290, HMSO, 1896.

Report of Inquiry by C. F. Masterman, MP, into Charges made concerning the Management of Heswell Nautical School, cd 5541, HMSO, 1911.

Report of the Departmental Committee on Reformatory and Industrial Schools, cd 8939, HMSO, 1913.

Report of the Child Adoption Committee, cmd 1254, HMSO, 1921.

Report of the Departmental Committee on the Treatment of Young Offenders, cmd 2831, HMSO, 1927.

Report on the Circumstances which led to the Boarding-Out of Dennis and Terence O'Neill at Bank Farm, Minsterley, and the Steps Taken to Supervise their Welfare (Monckton), cmd 6636, HMSO, 1945.

Report of the Care of Children Committee (Curtis), cmd 6922, HMSO, 1946.

Report of the Committee on Homeless Children (Clyde), cmd 6911, HMSO, 1946.

Sixth Report from the Select Committee on Estimates, Session 1951-2 (Child Care), HC 235, HMSO.

'Departmental Reply to the Sixth Report from the Select Committee on Estimates, Session 1951-2 (Child Care), appendix 1 to the *13th Report of the Select Committee on Estimates 1951-2,* HC 328, HMSO.

Report of the Committee on Children and Young Persons (Ingleby), cmd 1191, HMSO, 1960.

Disturbances at the Carlton Approved School on 29th and 30th August, 1959, Report of Inquiry by Mr Victor Durand, QC, cmd 937, HMSO, 1960.

Administration of Punishment at Court Lees Approved School, Report of Inquiry by Mr Edward Gibbens, QC, cmnd 3367, HMSO, 1967.

Report of the Committee on Local Authority and Allied Personal Social Services (Seebohm), cmnd 3703, HMSO, 1968.

Report of the Departmental Committee on the Adoption of Children (Houghton), cmnd 5107, HMSO, 1972.

Report of the Committee of Inquiry into the Care and Supervision Provided in Relation to Maria Colwell, HMSO, 1974.

Department of the Environment, District Audit, *The Provision of Child Care: A Study of Eight Local Authorities in England and Wales – Final Report,* HMSO, 1981.

A Child in Trust: the Report of the Panel of Inquiry into the Circumstances Surrounding the Death of Jasmine Beckford, London Borough of Brent, 1985.

Report of the Inquiry into Child Abuse in Cleveland, 1987, cm 412, HMSO, 1988.

Government and other sources

Board of Supervision and Local Government Board for Scotland, *Annual Reports.*

Ministry of Health, *Annual Reports.*

Home Office, *Reports on the Work of the Children's Branch* (later Children's Department).

Home Office (then Department of Health and Social Security, now Department of Health), *Children in the Care of Local Authorities in England and Wales.*

Local Government Board (formerly Poor Law Board), *Annual Reports.*

Reformatory and Industrial Schools, *Annual Reports of the Inspector.*

Barnardo's, *Annual Reports.*

The Catholic Directory, Universe Publications.

National Children's Home, *Annual Reports.*

The Waifs and Strays Society, *Annual Reports.*